INFLIGH

E

MW00876574

http://www.facebook.com/inflightentertainmentbook

http://www.inflightentertainmentbook.com

CONTENTS

PREFACE

The community of flight attendants (F/A or F/A's) is quite a close-knit one and events that happen on one side of the world are fodder for *jump-seat* gossip on the other side of the world mere hours after they occur. In fact it has been said there are three forms of mass communications: telephone, telegraph and tell a flight attendant!

Consequently, many of things that happened to me in the course of my flying career have entered the lexicon of F/A folklore as *urban legends*. However, I can assure you that even though variations of my stories have been repeated from F/A to F/A; many times details changed in the re-telling - these events actually occurred to me!

One of the advantages of being a *senior* F/A is that by virtue of having been around for four decades I have seen and done everything under the sun. For a lot of us, we were witness to more than our share of outrageous and ludicrous events; and more often than not were first hand witnesses to inflight insanity.

PROLOGUE

Back in the good ol' bad days before political correctness gave such nicknames a bad rap and before the ravages of time caught up with me, I was a dedicated party animal. Like millions of twenty-somethings before me, I believed I was invincible. Given the fact that I had the world's best nightclubs as a playground (and the use of recreational substances was prevalent in those days), I'm grateful to be above ground today. That being said, you never know when your inglorious past can return to taunt, if not haunt you.

Several years had passed since I had laid waste to the wild nightlife of Waikiki, Honolulu. A typical layover involved staggering back to the hotel mere hours to go before pick-up; dark glasses protecting my blood-shot eyes, clothing disheveled, hair a wreck and balancing a large piping hot black coffee ... in each hand. This was the first step in resurrecting myself for the return flight home. I often passed the same vendors and shop keepers on my pre-dawn exodus which I affectionately referred to as the *walk of shame*. One lady in particular always seemed to be opening her vintage Hawaiian shirt store, a favorite haunt of mine, as I made my un-steady way home. She would cheerfully greet me with the same refrain, before gleefully sending me on my way "Aloha, did you bring Auntie her coffee this morning?"

Imagine my surprise, when over a decade later, I was sedately making my way (soberly I might add) along Waikiki's main street in the early afternoon only to be greeted with, "Eh! Two cups! How's by you my brotha?" Startled, I looked up into the smiling face of the woman whose shop I had stumbled by all those years earlier. Laughing boisterously I assured her that those days were well past me and that these days ONE cup of coffee was all that was needed to start my day!

CHAPTER 1

CHANGE OF DIRECTION

It's true; a change in the weather can change your life. A raging mid-western blizzard complete with driving snow and horizontal sheets of ice, had kept me captive in the fraternity house I was living in on a frigid February day of my senior year in university.

With my own grade point average on a solid course for graduation with honours, I had forged a lucrative business ghost-writing term papers for bored jocks with quite a lot of brawn but decidedly deficient in brains.

That snowy afternoon, I was sitting in an alcove window seat, immersed in Dickens for a senior basketball star, when I noticed a woman, smartly dressed in a distinctive blue coat and matching bowler hat, take a spectacular pratfall on the sidewalk directly in front of the frat house. Dashing out into the elements to come to the aid of the stylish stranger, I lifted her up and retrieved her purse and hat. To my surprise this damsel in distress turned out to be a close friend who had graduated just the year before. After expressing my joy and surprise at our unexpected reunion, I asked Leslie what she was doing on campus, and more importantly, just why she was dressed in a bowler hat and white gloves especially in a snowstorm!

Leslie explained that she was in town to recruit flight attendant F/A applicants for Pan American Airways (Pan Am). She told me she was *based* at JFK in NYC and had just returned from a four-day layover in Rio and that her next scheduled flight was to London, the first leg of a trip that would literally take her around the world. When my mouth had closed, I asked her, "Where do I sign up?" Visions of pristine beaches and foreign ports firmly planted in my mind.

By this time, five of my fraternity brothers had shown up and catching wind of what Leslie was doing, they too expressed a deep desire to *see the world* from 39,000 feet. After Leslie's description of the places she had visited and the incredible people she had met, it took very little convincing for the other five to want to sign up also for the initial interview with Pan Am.

Bill, a strapping jock, Toby, our resident geek, Hunter, an overweight party animal, Jeffrey and Jordan, identical twins, and I all decided to try our luck at the open-house introduction to be held at the student union. Resplendent in her Pan Am blue gabardine skirt and form-fitting jacket and sky-high heels, Leslie looked every inch the part of the exotic sexy stewardess as she held court in her bowler hat and crisp white gloves, regaling a rapt (and slightly awed) student body with her tales of far-flung ports and first class cabins strewn with stars, fashion icons and recording artists. All six of us were ready for global adventures. I was open to an exciting summer of travel having been accepted for Law School and figured that I had nothing to lose by working for a major airline before I began further study for an upcoming career in law.

A few weeks later the student union was the scene of a large-scale interview, which was then narrowed to applicants who would be contacted for a more personal, one-on-one interview. As one of the lucky recipients of a *call-back* interview, I found myself ushered into a suite in one of the most prestigious hotels in town. Pan Am stipulated that all of its F/A's were not only college graduates, but fluent in at least one foreign language. I awaited my interview quietly giving thanks that I was fluent in French and had remained up-to-date in all of my university French classes.

My interview was conducted by a pair of statuesque Nordic ice-maidens who in classic *good cop/bad cop* mode, took turns with one making unwavering eye contact, while the other (furiously taking notes) kept her focus solely on a notepad where she recorded our interaction.

Bemused at first, then increasingly frustrated by what I perceived as studied ennui, I found my nervousness had dissipated and was replaced by a sense of self-assurance and confidence. After all, I still had Law School in my immediate future as *plan A*. Forty minutes later the interview was over. Half of that time had been conducted in rapid-fire French and then I was out the door, rushing to a lecture, daydreams of continent-hopping banished from my head.

One month before graduation a telegram arrived for me at the frat house. Having never received one before, my first thought was a queasy one; who had died? Trepidation turned to elation as I read: *Pan American World Airways is pleased to inform you that you have been accepted as a member of our flight service training class to begin on May 10.*

As luck would have it, graduation was on May 2. My *summer adventure* was about to become a reality.

CHAPTER 2

TRAINING DAYS

I stepped off the plane in Miami, a freshly-minted college graduate eager to embark on a six-week training regime to become a member of Pan Am's elite cabin crew. As I did so I was immediately struck by the intense humidity and tropical heat and the incredible diversity of Miami's citizens. Having been raised in the upper Midwest in a cold climate and hearing few if any foreign languages spoken with regularity, I experienced this polyglot metropolis as an immediate culture shock.

After checking into the hotel, which was to be my home for the next six weeks, I strolled across the broad avenue and into the imposing gardens of Pan Am's Art Deco-inspired training facilities. It was here, standing in front of a magnificent reflective pool, that I made the acquaintance of someone who would become my life-long friend.

Elaine White was a vivacious, extremely poised and attractive young lady from the East Coast, who, like me, had recently graduated from university but was in the class ahead of mine in training. Bonding over a shared disgust at the tennis ball-sized flying roaches (ugh!), Elaine gave me the succinct and pertinent advice that would serve me in good stead for the next six weeks, "Keep your eyes open, a smile on your face and your mind on your inflight manual and you'll be just fine".

She also informed me which pitfalls to avoid while undergoing the constant scrutiny required to metamorphose from clever neophyte to the cultured and world-wise F/A Pan Am had stated its vaunted reputation upon.

That evening I met the incredibly diverse group of people who would comprise the 22 members of my training class. There were seven men in our group, which would make us novices in what had been, since WWII, the province of women only.

As male F/As we were in the vanguard of what was once the exclusive domain of nubile young women. I must admit we were quite pleased with ourselves to be the *foxes amongst the hens.*

My class included representatives from Norway, Sweden, England, Ireland, Scotland, France, Italy and two striking beauties from South Africa; one of which was the first black African to join Pan Am's family. It was truly amazing to interact with this mini United Nation (UN) when we had our F/A orientation.

In hindsight, our group closely resembled a glossy print for the United Colours of Benetton, however, Pan Am adhered to a strict code of appearance and as attractive as we believed ourselves to be, our instructor viewed us as diamonds in the rough. Pan Am's first task was to transform us into airborne professionals.

In those days, I liked to think that I was the epitome of the current style, sporting a huge Jackson Five 'fro and clothing straight out of Miami Vice. Of course that look didn't fly with the cadre of instructors determined to mould a group of peons into polished, sophisticates worthy of the *World's Most Experienced Airline.*

The first thing to undergo radical change was my *'do'.* I went from urban chic to chairman of the board with a modest trim. Each of us underwent a complete makeover and by the end of our first week we began to take on, outwardly at least, a patina of sophistication.

Our days were spent learning the safety procedures of Pan Am's fleet of aircraft, the most important aspect of our training, and mastering the intricacies of the presentation and delivery of haute cuisine at 39,000 feet. It may seem difficult to believe, but once upon a time airlines provided passengers with meals served on fine china accompanied by a vast selection of fine wines!

Even those passengers travelling in coach were offered a selection of meals that seem extravagant today. Coq-au-vin, veal cutlets, braised lamb chops; they were standard offerings back in those days.

The only down side to these culinary delights was the fact that we were actually expected to *cook* these meals on board. Previous to this shock to my system my expertise in the kitchen, or *galley* as it is known in an aircraft, was pouring milk over cereal. Needless to say I was a rapt if not a terrified student during our galley training courses.

My roommates did not fare as well, literally burning every meal they attempted to prepare; no doubt due to their marijuana induced haze.

The one course I was looking forward to was our immersion in bartending. We were expected to know which wines were best enjoyed with whatever food we served, in addition to being able to concoct numerous cocktails. The bonus to this was that we were allowed to *sip* our finished products, something we all thoroughly enjoyed.

As the weeks passed, our ranks were thinned out by a process of elimination. This was in the days before political correctness and Pan Am had a strict weight and appearance policy. One of the men and two of the girls were dismissed for not complying with the weight requirements expected of cabin crew, the most memorable of which being one young lady who, while on her familiarisation flight, fell onto and collapsed the dessert cart in first class, all the while stuffing her face with pastries.

Finally, the day to which we had all been looking forward arrived and on graduation day 16 beaming brand new F/As had their wings pinned on their uniforms by a senior vice president of Pan Am.

It was with an immense sense of pride and accomplishment that we posed for our class photo. Each of us was pleased that the world was now our oyster!

Graduation. Can you spot me?

Pan Am maintained base cities at JFK (New York), MIA (Miami), LAX (Los Angeles), SFO (San Francisco), SEA (Seattle), HNL (Honolulu), LHR (London) and (FRA) Frankfurt.

That afternoon, we drew slips of paper from a stewardess's bowler hat which would determine where our base city would be. When my turn came I selected JFK and let out a whoop of joy. I was headed for the *big bad apple* and was more than prepared to set the world on fire.

CHAPTER 3

BIG APPLE

New York! Both the city and its inhabitants tend to put everyone in their place. Everything is bigger, brighter and more exciting than any other metropolis on the planet. The same analogy applied to the crews based at JFK, the major hub for Pan Am.

When I reported for duty for my very first flight as working crew, I was overwhelmed by the sight of hordes of *Glamazons*, all immaculately clad and coiffed, bustling through the terminal. The many languages spoken made it seem more like the floor of the United Nations than an airline lounge as I nervously tried to locate the briefing room for Flight One to London's Heathrow airport.

A briefing is held before every flight conducted by the chief purser and the pilot in command of the fight. When I entered the room assigned to the London flight, a tall, slender German woman was standing at a podium holding a glove in one hand while gesticulating with blood red talons on the other. Her pallid complexion was offset by a short raven-haired bob and her mouth was a vermilion slash of scorn. She would not have been miscast as the stern and overbearing warden in a woman's correctional facility.

Her eyes narrowed as she spied me trying to make myself as small and as inconspicuous possible and slid into the seat nearest the door.

Glaring at me she growled in a gravelly baritone, "Vell girls... what have ve got here??? Mein Gaht... a MAHN!" I doubt that I was successful at keeping my knees from knocking together when she asked my name. This was the infamous Hildegard Heinemann, notorious for being one of Pan Am's strict and by-the-book pursers.

Hildegard took a dramatic drag from her cigarette and exhaling pronounced in a voice like doom that, "YOU ... vill be .... vorking vith me". I paid attention to the little voice inside my head that squeaked, "I am completely and totally SCREWED!"

Throughout the flight to London, I felt like the cornered prey of a hawk as Hildegard's beady eyes followed my every movement on the plane. My stomach was in a constant state of flux whenever I inadvertently caught her attention. My nervousness was exasperated by the fact that the first class cabin was filled with VIPs, most notably the ambassador from Nigeria, who was on his way to deliver a major address to the world health conference being held in London.

The ambassador was busy perusing a speech that he had just written in fountain pen when the beverage service began. I had a tray which contained six full champagne flutes I was delivering throughout the cabin. At the exact moment I was pulling out his tray table to place his drink on it we hit turbulence and the entire contents of my tray including the six full glasses of champagne were spilled not only on his stack of papers but also over his shirt, tie and pants.

Horrified, I gasped like a just-hooked fish as the ambassador waving his now sodden and ineligible speech in my face yelled, "YOU IMBECILE! Look what you have done!"

I was in the process of offering a mortified apology while simultaneously mopping up the mess I had caused when Hildegard swooped down the aisle, with eyes blazing, headed in my direction.

I would like to think that fear was the culprit for as Hildegard approached me, her arm raised towards the rear of the plane and hissed one word, "GO!" my upset stomach rebelled and I let out a loud and very theatrical burst of flatulence. I hastily retreated to the relative anonymity of coach all the while being pursued by peals of laughter from the cabin I had just vacated.

CHAPTER 4

GRACE UNDER PRESSURE

Experience and time soon helped to diminish my first flight debacle into a dim but persistent memory. Six months later I was relieved to find myself just days from ending my probationary status and becoming a fully-fledged F/A.

Because Pan Am was a worldwide carrier, I had been to practically every major city in the world in just a few months and could not believe my good fortune. Having successfully escaped the clutches of Hildegard Heinemann, I had settled into the routine schedule of a *junior* F/A working in the coach cabin of the 747 aircraft. The amount of time you accrued in the airline determined your seniority, or lack thereof. Junior F/As with the least amount of seniority generally worked in the coach cabin of each aircraft.

Flight 73 from Frankfurt to JFK was on final approach after the purser had made the announcement to prepare the cabin for landing. I was instructing the passengers in the last cabin where I was working to bring their seatbacks into the upright position and stow their tray tables in preparation for an imminent landing.

As I approached the very last row and my jump seat, I came across a heavy set German girl sprawled as far back as her seat would allow, panting and looking extremely distressed. When I told her that she had to bring her seat to an upright position she looked me frantically in the eyes and shouted, "I can't... my water just broke!"

Clueless as to what she was referring to or just what this implied, I replied, "Lady, I will bring you another glass of water when we land but right now ...."

Stunned I glanced down and immediately grasped her predicament. I believe my exact words were "Holy shit" and I lunged for the phone at my jump seat. I made an emergency call to the purser who in turn made a call to the cockpit.

An inquiry went out across the PA system requesting a physician or anyone with medical training but we received no response.

By this time the captain had determined the best chance of getting our pregnant passenger help was to land ASAP and he proceeded to make a very deliberate and gradual decent. With the help of a couple of returning servicemen we managed to place our now apparent mother-to-be on the floor between the lavatories in the rear of the plane. My flying partner had arrived with the first aid kit but catching sight of the now screaming woman she bolted into the nearest lavatory locking herself in.

At this point, I have to stipulate that the closest I had ever come to witnessing childbirth was a decidedly chaste video we had been shown in training. Trust me, this real life event was as far from that sanitised piece of fluff as possible. In the annals of eye-opening experiences this was the top of the chart! There was no time for the clichéd *boiling of water* or any other niceties. Hastily placed blankets and the gloves from the first aid kit were all we had time for.

With the help of a woman that had been sitting next to her (and fortunately a mother of five!) who shouted words of encouragement like, "PUSH...SHUT UP AND PUSH!"

I tried to remain focused on the task at hand all the while looking bug-eyed at the scene unfolding in front of me. I assumed a catcher stance and 55 minutes later, after we had gingerly touched down, I caught the head, shoulders and glistening body of a baby girl as she made her dramatic entrance into the world. I had no idea what to expect so the ensuing bodily functions left me completely shell shocked.

Fortunately by now, we had taxied to the gate and six of New York's firemen and policemen came aboard and took over. The rest of the passengers were held back and, to a hearty round of applause, the new mother and daughter were taken off the plane via the aft door to a waiting ambulance and on to the hospital.

I found out later that both mother and daughter were in excellent health and the six-pound bundle of joy had been named apparently without any irony Pamela Anne. The next day, I was officially a fully-fledged F/A and received the first of many commendations.

I think I can safely state that the end of my probation had truly been a *baptism of fire*!

The thorn amongst the roses!

CHAPTER 5

TOKYO EXPRESS

As well as honing my skills in interacting with passengers, the difficult crazy ones as well as some incredible folks, I was also perfecting the minutiae of becoming a F/A.

First and foremost of the gems of wisdom necessary to be learned was the fine art of bidding, the process by which your monthly schedule is determined.

Junior F/As are at the bottom of the seniority list (the manner in which you are awarded flights) and as such had to bid every available line of flying to get a decent line or schedule. In addition, every junior F/A had to serve a month of stand-by, in which you were to remain on phone contact on the chance that someone did not show up for a flight or called in sick. This being well before the advent of cell phones, stand-by basically meant that you were held captive in your apartment, sometimes for hours on end, waiting for the phone to ring. Being based in JFK meant that you could theoretically be *called out* for a flight to any destination in the world.

I was serving my month of standby when I got a short call-out to replace a F/A on the trip to Tokyo. I dashed from my apartment in mid-Manhattan and headed to the Pan Am building over Grand Central Station to board the helicopter on the roof of that iconic structure for a 15-minute flight to JFK.

I must admit few jobs offered a more glamorous commute and riding the copter never lost its thrill for me. After checking in with the crew desk I reported for the briefing for the flight to Tokyo. This flight was operated on a Boeing 707 and made a 24-hour layover in Fairbanks, Alaska. Of course I was stoked to be a member of this quite senior crew, my excitement only abated by the fact that I was assigned the First Class galley. Given my limited culinary experience,

I was nervous but nevertheless confident that I could handle the job at hand.

Pan Am was famous for its on-board meals and deservedly so. I was expected to prepare, from scratch, lobster thermidor, braised lamb chops, Dover sole and roast sirloin to perfection. The meals were served on linen-lined carts and were extravagant in their presentation. Each course was delivered with panache; caviar, oysters Rockefeller and chilled vodka followed by canapés and a soup course. As I said, this was a different world and time.

On the Fairbanks flight the *piece-de-resistance* was a flaming baked Alaska dessert dramatically lit in blue flames and wheeled down the aisle and served by a white-jacketed purser.

Like the Wizard of Oz, I was the *little man behind the curtains* frantically trying to prepare and plate these masterpieces and set up the next cart as the meal service progressed.

With a little coaching and words of wisdom from my co-workers in First Class working the aisle positions, blessedly everything went off without a hitch.

Breakfast was another story altogether. I was faced with the dilemma of cooking eggs to order for the 14 passengers seated in the cabin. I was extremely worried about preparing eggs over easy, sunny side up or omelettes when I had an ingenious solution. As soon as the purser was not looking I went through the cabin and asked passengers just how they like their scrambled eggs prepared: soft, medium or hard. I accomplished this without anyone being the wiser, or upset with the consistency of their scrambled eggs!

My first foray into Alaska is indelibly imbedded in my memory. This was in the month of February and as soon as we de-planed, we were given fur-lined parkas to wear during our 24-hour layover in Fairbanks. The air was bracingly crisp and bitingly cold; the snow-laden landscape breathtakingly beautiful. By far the most spectacular aspect of that trip was the awesome display of the

Aurora Borealis, the northern lights dancing a staccato fandango in the Alaskan sky.

At that time, the main terminal of the Fairbanks airport contained a 12-foot polar bear, rearing up and its claws extended in attack mode. Even though stuffed, it remained a ferocious reminder of Alaskan wildlife.

The crew hotel was an authentic rustic log cabin complete with a roaring fireplace in the lobby. After meeting up with the crew for a debriefing, hot toddies around the fireplace, I retired to my room leaving the curtains parted so I could watch the magic show in the sky. As I lapsed into sleep I heard the distant but distinct call of wolves and reminded myself what a grand adventure my life had become.

Tokyo from the air was a revelation. Its neon-lit towering skyscrapers brought to mind Manhattan, but the majestic silhouette of Mt Fuji looming on the horizon gave it a romantic grace all of its own. I had four days in which to sightsee and immerse myself in one of the most cosmopolitan and exciting cities in the world. My first impression of Tokyo was how completely the modern world meshed with the past; blue suited businessmen together with kimono clad women dashing about in a mad pursuit of industry. Tokyo is one of the most stylish and fashion-forward cities in the world and the juxtaposition of traditional Japan and *haute couture* was amazing to behold. Because of the large population, co-operation among the citizens is not only a necessity but also an art form of civility in itself.

We were wandering the wide plazas around Shinjuku where we were staying when I came across a group of 12 blonde and bronzed gorgeous creatures, obviously a group of some kind, taking in the sites. I asked the crewmember I was travelling with if they were models on a shoot but she informed me that they were members of Qantas, Australia's flagship-carrier.

I was still agog and admiring them as they came within hearing distance when one of the leggy blondes opened her mouth and in a voice like a choked chicken squawked, "Oi...Nolene, what'r youse doin fa tee?" A cat's claws on chalk board would have sounded musical when compared to the braying emitting from this beauty's mouth. I did not know it at the time but this lovely *sheila* was merely enquiring about what her mates were planning to do for dinner.

The chief purser on my Tokyo crew was fluent in Japanese and he took it upon himself to further my awareness of Japanese culture by taking me to a traditional tea ceremony. This is an extremely ritualistic tea pouring ceremony performed by kimono-clad women while playing the Shamisen, a Japanese lute. Each placement of the delicate porcelain cups and stylised movement is steeped in tradition. You are served while being seated at a very low table, your knees tucked under you in a yogic position.

Unfortunately, earlier in the evening, I had my first encounter with sake and it seemingly agreed quite well with me. Two bottles later we headed for the tea house and I was feeling absolutely no pain while assuming this position for what seemed like hours on end but it did nothing for either my equilibrium or my bladder.

The ceremony was nearing the end when I urgently and positively had to pee. Lurching my way upwards in what I thought was a graceful attempt to rise, I pitched sideways and rolled completely through the rice paper wall of our dining area and sprawled across the table of the Japanese patrons in the adjoining room knocking tea trays and sending crockery flying everywhere! Amid shrieks and heated remarks aimed at moronic Gaijin (foreigners) I stumbled to my feet slurring abject apologies. With the aid of my flying partners I lurched ungracefully into the night leaving a trail of destruction behind.

The Keio Plaza Intercontinental in Shinjuku is a stunning 32-storey glass and steel monolith that was our layover hotel in Tokyo.

I had taken a day trip to Kyoto with Brenda Bagsly, a fellow crewmember and one of the most delightful people it has been my privilege to meet in my life. We spent a fantastic day touring the medieval city, its castle, world-renowned gardens and the famous Geisha district.

Returning to Tokyo via the bullet train was an adventure in itself. The lush countryside, blazing by at 200 miles per hour, far more satisfying than being couped up in an aluminium tube for 13 plus hours at 39,000 feet. With a spectacular sunset as a backdrop, we arrived back in Tokyo for a pleasant dinner and retired to our rooms having made plans to tour the Imperial Gardens the following day.

Brenda's room was directly across from mine on the 26th floor. Around 5am I awoke to a violent shaking and rolling sensation and was thrown from my bed to the floor. My foggy mind snapped immediately to attention with the realisation that this was in fact a major earthquake (at least major to me).

Everything I had heard about being in such a situation involved locating the nearest exit to the room and standing in the doorframe. I had the presence of mind to don my kimono and wrenched open the door to my room, bracing myself in the framework of the door. Seconds later, Brenda, screaming loudly and calling on Jesus, slammed her door open. She was standing completely naked, her legs akimbo, her arms raised above her head and her breasts swinging like a metronome with each movement of the building. She screamed, "LORD JESUS!!! WHAT SHOULD WE DO?" Composing myself I shouted back, "If I were you I would start by covering my shit up!"

The shaking subsided as suddenly as it had begun and Brenda grabbed her kimono and we joined the other guests milling about the hallway, amazed that we had come through unscathed.

I will never forget my first encounter with an earthquake and *Miss B's* pneumatic peep show and the laughs we shared about that experience for years to come.

Brenda Bagsly.

CHAPTER 6

BACK TO MY ROOTS

The flight-scheduling department was the lifeline to the world for Pan Am F/As. The head scheduler was an affable and outgoing West Indian named Winston, who always had a cheerful disposition and a pleasant quip to pass on whenever he spoke to you.

Flight scheduling was situated next to the crew desk where we had to check in before each flight, and most days, Winston was there greeting F/As and wishing them bon voyage as they headed to their destinations. It had come to my attention that Winston enjoyed Cuban cigars and 100 proof Jamaican rum, so whenever I had the chance I purchased a present for him, not necessarily to curry his favour (well perhaps just a little!), but because he was a genuinely nice man. The dividend to becoming friendly with Winston was that I was more likely to be called out for more desirable flights in the months I served as standby crew.

Africa and flights to every major capital city on that continent were definitely some of the most popular and thus senior trips Pan Am operated out of JFK. The trip to Monrovia in Liberia, Accra in Ghana, Dakar in Senegal, Nairobi in Kenya and Johannesburg in South Africa was a 22-day affair with at least four days layover in each city. Most of the girls who worked this trip were Scandinavian goddesses and as such were known throughout the system as *The African Queens!* The nickname was not only a homage to Katherine Hepburn, but underscored the fact that these divas flew this trip almost exclusively and considered the route sacrosanct and their personal domain.

When Winston called me to report for a trip to the West Coast of Africa, I was therefore ecstatic and hastily prepared for my first sortie to that continent. I dashed off the helicopter and reported in early for the trip excited to be finally headed for what was my most exotic destination to date. I was seated in briefing and getting acquainted with my flying partners when I heard rather than saw the final crew member who would make up our group.

Hearing heels beating a frantic staccato on the tiled floor, I glanced up in time to witness a whirl-wind of activity just outside the door to the room in which we were gathered. Running at a full trot frantically applying lipstick, adjusting her bowler hat while simultaneously borrowing white gloves from an off duty F/A, she burst into the briefing.

When this tornadic activity had subsided, this dervish coalesced into the form of Ann-Marie Berry who was destined to become a lifelong friend and confidant. After the dust had settled and she regained her breath Ann-Marie gave everyone a dazzling smile and blithely chirped, "Sorry to be late!" a phrase that would be synonymous with her for as long as I have had the pleasure of her company.

Ann-Marie was a recent graduate of Berkeley and was as sharp-witted and clever as she was beautiful.

On that flight to Africa we forged a lifelong bond of friendship and discovered a mutual affinity for anything whatsoever to do with shopping. In 22 days, I learnt a lot about Ann-Marie but chief among her impressive resume was the fact that she was connected to some very important people, the movers and shakers of African society. Being both bright and beautiful had given her access and cache into all of the best places and people in Africa, an introduction I was more than pleased to share.

Ann-Marie

My first impression of Africa from the air was amazement at the verdant beauty spread out below. The years of movies and National Geographic photographic features that I had experienced, were pale comparisons to the lush jungles and sparkling rivers shimmering like vibrant jewels beneath us.

The second memory implanted in my mind was of the equatorial temperature, an instantaneous blast of palpable heat that hit like a brick wall as soon as the door of the plane was opened. Even though I knew they were acclimatized to the heat and humidity, I was amazed that our African passengers, especially the women who were dressed in full-length, colourful wraps and head dresses, could tolerate the scorching heat outside.

When we landed in Nairobi, our aircraft had not yet hooked up to the auxiliary power unit and consequently the aircraft had no air-conditioning while we were on the ground. All the members of the cabin crew had gathered at the forward entrance door and were fanning ourselves with the oversized first class menus when a woman in full African attire, head wrap and long colourful wrap skirt, burst through the curtain dividing the First Class cabin from economy, and shouted, "WHAT'S WRONG WITH THE PLANE...? WHAT'S WRONG?"

I was about to explain our mechanical situation when she interrupted me by declaring, "Do something quick... BECAUSE MY PUSSY ON FIRE!" I can guarantee our shrieks of laughter could be heard throughout the plane and I tried to assume a modicum of sincerity as I assured her that we would do everything we could to alleviate her problem.

After landing, we removed our jackets and standing around in shirt sleeves, we proceeded to remove every cold beverage within sight from the aircraft's coolers in preparation for the limo ride to the hotel. Refreshed by the copious consumption of *adult beverages*, we were fortified against the heat and eager to begin our African adventure.

Ann-Marie's contacts included several wealthy businessmen and shortly after checking into our hotel we found ourselves sprawled on the deck of a yacht, champagne flutes in hand, toasting the glamorous life.

That first trip was a whirlwind of parties, dancing, drinking, even more drinking and exploring the bazaars of Liberia, Ghana, Nairobi and Dakar.

On the second leg of the trip, Ann-Marie had charmed the host of a sprawling estate into taking us on a safari; in his custom fitted Lincoln limousine. The outrageous irony of two young African Americans being chauffeured around the lush veldt was not lost on us as we photographed wildlife from the moon roof of the limousine, all the while imbibing ridiculous amounts of champagne.

I had just purchased my first real piece of photographic equipment, a Nikon, and had wandered about 20 feet from the vehicle, when I spotted a couple of adorable lion cubs sleeping under a bush. I was busy snapping away when two things occurred simultaneously: I noticed a lioness crouched not too far from where I was standing, getting ready to protect her cubs; and I heard Ann-Marie and the driver screaming at me, "Move your ass… and get the hell out of there!"

I have amazing photos of the cubs, the quickly approaching lioness and the ground at every angle as the speed-shooting mechanism took over while I sprinted for the safety of the car. As we sped off, I got one last shot of the lioness, tail twitching, and then we quickly disappeared into the distance.

Mamma protecting her babies!

Completely engrossed in our luxurious picnic/safari, we found the day had slipped away from us.

By the time we had finished our third or fourth bottle of champagne, we suddenly realised that we had less than an hour until the departure of our flight to Dakar and we were literally in the middle of nowhere, miles away from our hotel and the airport.

We went from absolute panic to stone-cold sobriety in a matter of seconds, all the while exhorting our driver to break world land-speed records as we careened over dirt-packed roads through the jungle. We arrived back at the airport with only minutes to spare. By now I was sweating profusely as well as nauseous from the limo, a vehicle not at all suitable for the African bush. Foremost in our minds was the demise of our extremely short-lived flying careers and just how we were going to explain how we had managed to miss the continuation of our trip after a four-day layover in Nairobi.

Fortunately for us, Ann-Marie had befriended the airport station manager in Kenya and he allowed us to speed on to the tarmac, the limo screeching to a halt a few feet from the air stairs to the plane. The purser was screaming at us to get the "lead out of our asses" as we scrambled up the stairs to the forward entrance door, dishevelled and perspiring and still in safari attire (short-sleeve shirts and shorts).

We stumbled unceremoniously into the first class lounge of the 707, dazed and gasping for breath. We must have made a pathetic sight because Sonya, the Swedish purser, who moments before was attempting to admonish us burst into laughter, telling us to relax, the crew had assumed that we would be *running late* and had packed our bags and stowed them for us. I believe we both collapsed with relief as the plane taxied down the runway secure in the knowledge that our careers, if not our dignity, were still intact.

First steps on African soil.

CHAPTER 7

IN THE HOT SEAT

F/As are trained professionals who have been thoroughly trained to react to any emergency quickly, professionally and calmly.

In an emergency situation we revert back to immediate action mode, however, even sky gods have to come down from Olympus occasionally and admit to having feet of clay. My *Come to Jesus moment* occurred on the return flight from Ghana to Liberia during one of my African runs.

After preparing the cabin for landing in Roberts Field, Liberia, I was sitting in the First Class lounge with Cathy Connors, a bubbly wholesome all American girl from Chicago and a relatively new hire like myself. Cathy and I were making plans to join another group of young F/As in a beach-side barbeque where we planned to partake of some quality African *ganja* (marijuana) and chilled white wine. This was in the 80s in the days before drug-testing and occasional recreational smoking of joints was, although not the norm, were quite commonplace amongst F/As in their 20s.

From the altitude of the plane and the view from the lounge windows we could tell that we were on our final descent into Roberts Field. As Cathy and I strolled to our jump seats in the front of the cabin, we observed Svenska Hollestram, our chief purser, hurriedly exiting the cock-pit leaning against the door frame and crossing herself.

Svenska, a Swedish beauty famed for her calm demeanour as well as her particularly large assets, at that moment looked like the wrath of God; wide-eyed, hair dishevelled with a sheen of sweat marring her perfectly made-up face. At the same time as Cathy and I were exchanging worried glances, the plane began a rapid accent, pulling back up to the flight path and banking sharply to the right. Svenska, meanwhile, dashed into the First Class lavatory, slamming the door behind her.

Stunned, both Cathy and I thought she had gone completely crazy. While looking aghast at each other, we undid our seat belts and got on the planes inter-phone and asked permission to enter the cockpit to see just what the hell was going on.

Inside the cock-pit was a scene of controlled chaos; a grim-faced captain conferring with the control tower, the first officer and flight engineer both engaged in checking the myriad of dials and switches on the control panels.

When he had a moment to spare the flight engineer explained to us that Svenska had in fact saved the day. Something had not sounded or felt right to her and she had breached protocol by contacting the cockpit in the final stages of our descent. This proved fortuitous as the landing gear over the left wing had not lowered into its full down position, even though the cowling had opened.

At this moment the captain was completing a fly-by over the control tower to check if the gear was visible. When he received word that we did not have the landing gear fully lowered the captain had the flight engineer attempt to manually lower the wheel, and when that failed to work, made the decision to dump fuel and prepare for an emergency landing.

Even to well-seasoned travel professionals, these were the words that no F/A wants to hear. This dire situation was exacerbated by the fact that we were on a plane full to capacity with mostly first-time travellers whose collective demeanour would fall far short of being either calm, cool or collected!

As for the crew (most of whom like Cathy and myself had not been flying that long), even though we did our best to appear non-plussed, underneath our professional veneer we were all scared shitless! I can recall with clarity the look of sheer terror behind our un-blinking eyes as Svenska told us that we would have to prepare for a land evacuation.

Meanwhile, the pilots circled the airport dumping fuel, a procedure which could possibly take up to one or two hours. Loose bowel syndrome had indeed set-in.

After the initial shock of what was occurring had passed, our training kicked into over-drive and we set about our duties with grim determination. People have varying ways of coping with stressful situation and our crew was no different. Svenska, who snapped back into command mode, was a study in fortitude as she went through our emergency handbook, making certain we followed procedures to the letter. As for myself, I was a classic study of contrasts. Ever the consummate actor, outwardly I was stoic and went about my duties with a studied aplomb. Internally I was a nervous wreck. By the time we had to go through the cabin and brief the passengers, I was completely drenched in sweat and not the glowing variety, but the deep down wring-out-your underwear sweat of utter terror. I knew then what my mother meant when she admonished me to always wear clean underwear – just in case I was in an accident. But soak drenched under-clothes were the LEAST of my worries.

By now it was apparent to everyone on board that something was amiss, and pandemonium broke out when Svenska made her initial emergency announcement advising the passengers of our situation and more specifically, that we would be making an emergency landing without the use of the wheels underneath the right wing. The cabin was soon filled with imprecations and wails of "Jesus! Save us!" in several African dialects as well as heavily accented English. While people were obviously fearful, surprisingly no one panicked and every eye was on all of the F/As as we demonstrated the emergency exits, the position to place your body in to brace for impact and the commands we would use to exit the aircraft.

Our extensive training was apparent as we moved throughout the aircraft calmly reassuring everyone that all would be well, and moving passengers who would be of most assistance to us closer to the doors and window exits. The F/As were in the aisles and all was going according to plan until an elderly white woman, a missionary of some sort, took the opportunity to grab the microphone at the aft F/A jump seat to shriek out, "Prepare to meet Je...!" She never got to finish her sentence as she was pounced on by the aft galley F/A, who snatched the microphone from her and roughly ushered her back to her seat, uttering some very un-lady-like oaths in the process.

As clichéd as it sounds, time truly did crawl to a standstill and every single moment that passed by as we circled the area surrounding the airfield dumping fuel was an eternity of angst and trepidation. All of the tension was exacerbated by our ability to see the fire trucks alongside the runway below us.

My mind was reeling with the morbid thought that this could be the moment I *cashed in my ticket*. As I passed through the cabin while checking on our passengers' preparations, my mind became crystal clear and I channelled all of my fear into a single mantra that I repeated over and over to myself, "I WILL get OUT of this plane!"

Cathy and I were the two most junior of the crew and we were responsible for the over-window exits in the middle of the plane. Even though I had complete trust in the capabilities of our cockpit crew and was secure in the knowledge that the Boeing 707 was an incredible aircraft, I couldn't help but hypothesise that my chances of surviving an air crash while seated in the middle of the plane, as opposed to the tail or over the nose, were not promising. Even with that morbid thought creeping into my subconscious I repeated my mantra and was determined to make it out alive.

With 500 feet to go before impact Cathy and I assumed our brace positions at the over-wing exits all the while shouting for the passengers to, "Grab your Ankles, Grab your Ankles, Grab your Ankles!" We could hear the ground rapidly approaching and just moments before we made impact Cathy, who was wearing thick *Coca-Cola-lensed glasses*, glanced sideways at me and squealed, "Tal, my glasses! What if they fall off?" I peeked across at her and shouted, "Bitch, have you heard of Braille? FEEL your way out of this mother f...ker!"

Finally, with a horrifically loud thump, we bounced off the tarmac and briefly back up a few feet before careening to a halt, the plane listing slightly off-kilter on the right side where the gear had not deployed. The instant the captain's announcement to evacuate came across the loud-speaker both Cathy and I had wrenched our window exits open. I did not have time to complete the command to come this way before a surge of frenzied Africans were streaming out and over me in a mad dash to the edge of the wing and away from the plane.

I have never in my life witnessed so many large women move with such speed and agility. Miraculously, we evacuated the entire aircraft, 185 people in total, in less than two minutes. Several of the frantic passengers were seen to sprint not only away from the aircraft but through the terminal itself, hell bent on putting as much space between themselves and the plane as was humanly possible!

After making certain that no one was left on-board, our crew joined the passengers in beating a hasty retreat from our near disaster.

I have never felt such a surge of relief and appreciation for still being among the living. As soon as we were out of sight of the public, there were plenty of tears, both of exhaustion and jubilation, as we all marvelled at the drama that we had just lived through.

Later, after the completion of reports to both the Federal Aviation Administration (FAA) and the company, we literally celebrated as if there would be no tomorrow. After a boisterous night of shared emotional bonding, the sunrise the next morning was without doubt the most beautiful sight of my life.

CHAPTER 8

WORLD PEACE

Seat duplications (passengers assigned to the same seat) are a ubiquitous occurrence in the airline industry, and in the incipient days of computers happened quite frequently. Unless the flight was completely full, the F/As on board usually handled the situation by moving passengers to unoccupied seats.

We were about to depart Ghana for JFK when two Nigerian women, one with a child strapped in a colourful shawl on her back, got into a very agitated and very loud altercation involving an empty row of seats near the rear of the plane. Looking up the aisle, I glimpsed my flying partner, a diminutive red head from Ireland, eyes bulging in consternation as she peeped from behind the aft galley curtain. Assessing the situation and convincing myself that I could handle it alone I drew myself up to my full 5ft 8in and entered the fray.

As I approached the two women, things were rapidly escalating into a near brawl, the two literally getting into each other's faces shouting what I could only assume were threats of bodily harm. Although the dialect was unknown to me, the guttural clicks, slapping of faces and buttocks (their own thankfully!) and the fact that they had gathered up their dresses around their waists in preparation for battle spurred me to action. I dashed between them just as the woman with the baby strapped to her back was handing the child to a complete stranger across the aisle ordering him to "Hold my baby!" in order to engage her assailant in hand-to-hand combat. Heroically (or more foolishly!) placing myself between the two, I mediated a truce learning through hand gestures accompanied by furious clucking and clicking of tongues that they had both been assigned the same seat in that row. After a few minutes of frantic bartering on my part I negotiated a peaceful stalemate and escorted the woman travelling alone to a seat several rows in front of and far away from the enraged mother.

After I had collected the baby and returned him to his now calm and placated mother, the door to the aircraft was closed and we proceeded without further incident to JFK.

Had I been more enterprising I could have brokered tickets to what could have been a ten-round, knock-down *"THRILLER ON THE TARMAC"*. I often think back to that, "Hold my baby moment" and wonder why I wasn't nominated for the Noble Peace Prize that year.

CHAPTER 9

EXTRA CARGO

The flight home from JFK was enlivened by an unexpected passenger.

We were transporting live animals in our cargo hold which were all destined to be housed in the Philadelphia Zoo. Together with the chimpanzees and a female gorilla acquired for that zoo's breeding programme was a 20ft long python. While accessing the cargo hold to check on our precious cargo the flight engineer was stunned to notice that the container holding the snake was empty! A cursory examination of the cargo hold revealed that our slithery guest had found a way out of confinement and was now roaming free somewhere amongst the containers stored below deck.

Scrambling back to the cockpit, the flight engineer sheepishly informed the rest of the cockpit crew about our renegade reptile. As you can imagine this news flash was not well received. Even though this creature was non venomous, the thought that a large snake was loose on a 707 filled with unsuspecting passengers was NOT a comforting thought.

When the captain called us on the interphone and told the cabin crew to DISCREATELY search for our vagabond, I went ice-cold with fear. There are two creatures that literally give me a severe case of the CREEPS: spiders and snakes! After a half hour looking under sleeping passengers and in lavatories and in any out of the way place our runaway might be, one of the co-pilots spotted something moving languidly in the area just aft of the cargo containers in the plane's belly. When asked if I wouldn't mind helping to search the area, I reiterate, this was in the belly of the plane, I replied without hesitation, "I don't believe this was included in my job description and furthermore this was not what I had in mind when I signed up to join the airline!". As my momma always told me, "Honesty is the best policy".

Later on in the flight and as was expected, our runaway snake was discovered somewhere near his container. JFK Animal Control was informed and all ended well. Thanks be to God!

CHAPTER 10

SPICE TO THE MIX

The 1970s heralded a changing of the guard in the airline industry, and at Pan Am this was most dramatically highlighted by the hiring of minorities, myself included. In my case I was a double minority being not only African American but one of a handful of men to be employed as a flight attendant.

This mixture of minorities not only gave some much needed spice to an otherwise mainly European group of F/As but had the added benefit of adding some of the most beautiful women in the world to the roster of Pan-Am's legendary aircrews.

Yvonne Scheuer was a former Miss Jamaica whose quick wit, charm and intelligence were a perfect fit for her flawless beauty. I first met Yvonne on Pan-Am's Flight One, a 22-day excursion that would take us from JFK to London, Frankfurt, Beirut, Istanbul, Karachi, Tehran, New Delhi, Bangkok, Hong Kong, Tokyo and back to JFK. Having been hired a year or so before me, Yvonne kindly took me under her wing and assumed the mantle of guide, diplomatic attaché and den-mother.

Each step along our journey was highlighted by Yvonne dragging me through museums, flea-markets, bazaars and fabulous restaurants in each of the cities we had a layover in. Pan-Am had stressed to us that as representatives of America's premier flag-carrier, we should be impeccably dressed at all times and to be prepared for any occasion. Since we were on the road for such a great length of time, each of us had a considerable amount of luggage to haul around, which would have constituted a problem if not for the fact that we never had to handle our luggage. It was whisked from the plane to our hotel by porters at each city. This allowed Pan-Am girls to always look crisp and fresh, uniform pressed, hats at a jaunty angle, white gloves gleaming as they strolled through air terminals and Inter-Continental hotels throughout the globe.

One night in Istanbul Yvonne had commandeered a car and driver to take a group of us to her favourite seafood restaurant, which afforded a magnificent view of the twinkling lights of the Bosporus, the strait that forms the boundary between Europe and Asia. True to form Yvonne was dressed to the nines in an evening outfit that featured a thigh-hugging skin-tight skirt, her customary strand of pearls and assorted jewels and six inch stiletto Ferragamo heels.

As promised, the dinner was excellent, the wine perfection and the view from the balcony on which we dined superb. All went swimmingly until the end of the meal, when Yvonne excused herself to use the ladies' room. She had only been gone for a few minutes when the relative calm and chatter of the remaining diners was interrupted by an ear-piercing scream emitting from the toilet in which Yvonne had entered moments before. As one we rushed from the table, banged on the cubicle door and asked if she was alright. I should point out that in parts of the world, particularly in Asia, Western-style toilets are not the norm and holes placed in the floor serve as receptacles of waste. Not getting an immediate response we pushed open the door to be presented with the sight of Yvonne, skirt hiked-up around her waist, a brown vicious liquid (that was not her own!) staining her clothing as she was lodged firmly in the hole which served as the latrine.

To add insult to injury, she had broken off one of the heels of her outrageously expensive shoes, when she slipped on the slick floor, falling into the proverbial shit-hole in an attempt to answer nature's call. With a furious look on her face she shouted, "Don't just stand there! Help me get the fuck OUT of this hole!" With as much grace as she could conjure up under the circumstances and with the assistance of her three hysterically laughing companions, Yvonne managed to extricate herself out of her foul-smelling predicament.

After requisitioning a table cloth from the proprietor of the restaurant to wrap around her now soiled skirt and blouse and with as much dignity as she could muster, carrying her broken pumps in one hand, she made her was back to the hotel, in the back of a taxi, the rest of us crammed in to the front seat with a wary but extremely amused driver.

Rehydrating after a long flight!

CHAPTER 11

NEW POPE

When Pope John Paul I died, I was selected to work a charted 747 to Rome and the plane was filled with clerics and prominent Catholics from throughout the United States. Our first and business class cabins housed the leading cardinals and bishops, many of them dressed in business attire as opposed to clerical robes, who would be selecting the next Pope. Scattered amongst this august group were the leading television anchors and news reporters at that time.

I was standing at the front door of the aircraft greeting our First Class passengers with Claudia Tagalatoria, our Italian language qualified F/A and a devout Catholic. As each cardinal entered the plane Claudia dropped to her knees genuflecting and kissing their rings. As there were quite a few of these Princes of the Church on board, this went on for quite a while.

Peter Jennings, a handsome news anchor and rising star of ABC television, had just crossed the threshold of the first class cabin, when Claudia dropped to her knees and began kissing his ring. Instantly realizing her mistake, I hastily tried to explain who this distinguished and easily recognizable gentleman was, all the while attempting to get Claudia to release his right hand and university class ring. Mr Jennings, astonished at this display of fealty, grinned broadly and declared that this was absolutely the very best greeting he had received on any airline, EVER! The other bishops and cardinals burst into applause and raucous laughter congratulating the newsman on his instant elevation within the Church. It took her sometime to recover her composure and join in the laughter, but Claudia replied in both English as well as Italian, "I was covering all of my bases".

After a marvellous week spent sightseeing and eating my way through Rome, my trip was highlighted by witnessing the puff of white smoke in Saint Paul Square heralding the beginning of the papacy of Pope John Paul II.

The return flight from Rome was uneventful save for an amorous journalist who, emboldened by an overabundance of *vino rosso*, grabbed Claudia's derrière. In a scene straight out of a Fellini film, she whirled around and her face inches away from the inebriated Don Juan, let loose with language that would have put a stevedore to shame. Claudia's face actually became more scarlet than her luxurious mane of hair which tumbled about her face, Medusa-like, as she verbally castigated her by now cowering assailant.

Needless to say everyone within listening distance was on their very best behaviour for the remainder of the trip.

CHAPTER 12

ADVENTURES IN RIO

Rio de Janeiro, Brazil, was another of my favourite destinations. Flying into that spectacular bay and catching sight of Corcovado Mountain crowned by the 98-ft tall statue of Christ the Redeemer giving a benediction to the teeming masses spread out below never ceased to amaze me.

I have always been an aficionado of classic films, especially those of the 1930s and 1940s in which aviation featured a major role. *Flying down to Rio* which was filmed in 1933 starring Delores Del Rio, Fred Astaire and Ginger Rogers, showcased Pan Am's famed flying boats, the majestic aircraft that transported these stars to Rio. Sitting in the upper deck of a Boeing 747 Clipper Ship, taking in the wondrous sights of Corcovado Mountain for the first time, I was transported back to the glorious days of the flying boat carrying Fred and Ginger to one of the world's most fabulous cities.

A layover in Rio was an eagerly sought after trip and I was truly delighted when I was lucky enough to get assigned one. A member of our crew, Hazel Bowman, was a joyous bundle of energy and a prodigious tour guide to all of the sights, sounds and culinary delights that Rio had to offer. She was fluent in Portuguese and had amassed a treasure trove of information regarding the best places to eat, shop and play. We had barely reached our hotel before changing into swim suits and hitting the famed Copacabana beach. I can honestly say to this day that I had never laid eyes on a more beautiful scene of *sun-worshippers* in my life!

This was my first introduction to beach volleyball and the smallest swimsuits, on both sexes, that I had ever seen. For a puritanical straight-laced Midwestern boy in knee-length swim trunks, the amount of bronzed flesh on public display was mind-boggling. Sensory overload left me looking like a rube, mouth open and eyes boggling, wherever my eyes landed. My version of heaven would definitely have been modelled on the scene before me and I doubt if anything could have wiped the smile from my face.

Rio de Janeiro. One of the world's most beautiful cities.

A salsa beat is the perfect sound track to a city blessed with amazing topography that delights the senses and includes stunning beaches populated with amazingly attractive citizens and vast favelas teeming with people with boundless energy and a zest for life.

While our days were occupied with beach-combing (by now I had ditched my sensible swim shorts for the uniform speedo worn by the locals) and exploring the markets throughout the city for various treasures, our evenings were spent, literally, dancing the night away. After a few dusk to dawn excursions to dozens of nightclubs (known as discos at the time), I'd like to think that I had mastered a fair approximation of the samba. It is astounding just how dexterous one can become after an evening downing copious quantities of *Caipirinhas*.

Upon awakening in the early afternoon, we would gather by the lavish pool-side cabanas overlooking the shoreline and nurse our throbbing heads and relieve our sore feet from the previous night's excursions by feasting on freshly baked rolls and fruit indigenous to Brazil. As I mentioned earlier, by now we had all gone *native* and were sporting the most scandalous and revealing bathing suits imaginable and were enjoying both the sun and the perfect weather.

There were six of us in various modes of deshabille happily sipping our first *Caipirinhas* of the day, when I was approached by an older British gentleman who was fully clothed in a smartly wrinkled white linen suit. The contrast between our post-prandial group of revellers and the staid, quintessential English specimen could not have been more pronounced. He looked like a character out of a Graham Green novel sporting a Panama hat, tortoise shell round-rimmed glasses and a polka-dot bow tie. And this was midday in Brazil!

My first observation upon noticing him headed in my direction was, "Why is he dressed like that and what the hell could he possibly want with me?" He was carrying a cigar-sized box wrapped in brown paper and tied securely with twine. Smiling and in the voice of an Oxford don he inquired if I were part of the Pan Am aircrew. When I answered in the affirmative he very smoothly asked when I was departing Rio, if I was headed to New York and would I "perform a very small favour" for him by taking this parcel to a *nephew* who would meet me outside customs in JFK.

My exact thoughts at this request from a complete (over-dressed) stranger were, "WTF?" While I had indeed been born at night that particularly glorious event had not, in fact, occurred the night before! I glanced about me at my flying partners who, having over-heard our conversation, were now peering over their sunglasses with the same unmasked look of suspicion that must have been evident on my face.

 When I politely but strongly rebuffed his offer of monetary compensation for this *favor*, he changed tactics and assured me that the package was in fact a rare manuscript that he didn't trust to send by mail and that I was more than welcome to check the package myself, further assuring me that both he and his *nephew* would be most grateful for my assistance. At this point, several of my crew had determined that politesse was not going to deter our over-dressed friend and decided to vacate the premises immediately. My would-be benefactor made one more attempt to curry my favour, but I was more inclined to view the repercussions of smuggling whatever it was that parcel contained as far outweighing any benefits to me or the risk to my crew; well that and a strong abhorrence of an outfit that involved horizontal stripes and a snug six by four cell.

The blissful weather, the dazzling nightlife and serendipitous beaches notwithstanding, Rio was also famed for its outstanding cuisine! Hazel was our intrepid leader, blazing new trails on a culinary expedition throughout every neighborhood in town. Every meal was an adventure. From exquisite five-star restaurants whose patrons were dressed to the nines, to sidewalk cafes in the favelas – Hazel had scoured them all. As a consequence of her research we dined like royalty wherever we ventured.

After a particularly strenuous evening of downing *Caipirinhas* and dancing in the clubs (and eventually the streets!), we found our way to a picturesque little café tucked away in a side street in one of the more colorful favelas near Ipanema.

It was very early in the morning and we considered ourselves fortunate to have stumbled across an establishment that was still serving dinner. Over a bottle or two of a rather ordinary red wine we decided to order a large pot of Feijoada; a local delicacy which was comparable to a black bean stew. It contained a variety of salted pork and beef, bacon and smoked ribs, at least two types of sausage and jerked beef plus an assortment of vegetables and bananas. Of all the food I sampled in Rio, this masterpiece was by far my favorite.

In somewhat of a drunken orgy, we sat down and began to devour our still steaming, heaped bowls of Feijoada. We were the only patrons at this ungodly hour and we had the place to ourselves. I was snacking on a small rib bone (or so I thought) when I suddenly realized that the screeching sound that had imperceptibly been in the background was intensifying to a now distinct caterwauling shriek. Looking up from my bowl beside which there were now several small bones neatly discarded on a plate, I noticed several extremely scrawny and agitated alley cats clawing at the screen door opposite the kitchen in the rear of the café.

I glanced down at the small bones then back up in alarm at the cacophony of cats squawking their outrage at the screen door. Instantly rendered to a somewhat sober state, I put down my spoon and said, "Uh guys ... I think those cats are looking for their babies!" As one, all six of us looked down at the bowls of stew then at the frantic cats ... and pushed away from the table as fast as was humanly possible! It was most likely a drunken assumption; but the THOUGHT that we had been dining on *kitten stew* put a rapid end to our late night fiesta, and we dashed off into the night.

Rio, like many places around the world, is a city of vast contradictions; it has astounding wealth and beauty, surrounded by pockets of undeniable poverty and desperation. This dichotomy between those with the means to live a truly enjoyable lifestyle and those living below the poverty line is by no means limited to Brazil and can indeed be found in any city in America. However, having said that and not being a proponent of firearms in general, one of the most frightening experiences of my flying career occurred while on a return to the airport in Rio.

Our crew bus was halted at a traffic light awaiting the signal to change to green when we were swarmed by motorbikes on all sides. This in itself was disturbing enough, but when we realized that all of the bikes' occupants were masked and armed with what appeared to be small caliber hand guns, the fear factor escalated rapidly. When the leader of this group of bandits boarded our minibus waving his pistol and shouting obscenities in Portuguese, we immediately accepted our precarious position and hauled our asses out as quickly as we could. We needed no further incentive to comply even though none of the six addressed us in English; their brandished weapons were motive enough to do their bidding. I should note this would have been the perfect occasion for the invention of the adult-diaper as our collective bowels were instantly turned to jelly with fear!

This all happened within minutes and strangely it seemed that no other vehicles were in the vicinity of the road in which we were stranded. Once outside the minibus, we were ordered to stand facing the van with our hands in the air after which the thieves were able to make quick work of removing watches, wallets and any jewelry that was at hand. At the time I was wearing my first quality watch, a gold Seiko time piece with a red crocodile strap. It was one of the first purchases I had made for myself in Tokyo, and I was quite fond of it, but nevertheless handed it over without hesitation.

In the confusion that followed our crew being ordered off the bus, Hazel, who had only recently become engaged to a well-known film actor and was sporting a five carat emerald-cut tiffany diamond ring, managed to keep her wits about her and secreted the ring off her finger and into her panties. While she was relived of her gold Rolex, she was resourceful enough to save her most-valued possession by placing it in *nature's lock box*.

As she understood what was being said by these bastards, I mean bandits, she had ascertained that they were only out to rob and not shoot or maim us. However, at the time, I was intently focused on saving my ass; to hell with the jewelry!

After collecting their booty, the thieves fled into the hills on their bikes leaving a thoroughly shaken and numb group of F/As on the side of the road. Several hours later after contacting Pan Am headquarters in Rio and giving depositions to the local police we returned to the hotel. Our return flight had been postponed and another crew re-assigned to work our trip back to JFK.

The next day, somewhat calmer and rested, the first class cabin contained six emotionally drained but not entirely sober F/As, each one eager to return to the relative quiet and calm of that concrete jungle; New York City. When I spotted the Statue of Liberty from the plane's window, I remember thinking and, to paraphrase the words of Dorothy in *Wizard of Oz* - "Baby, there's no place like home!"

CHAPTER 13

BOSTON BLUE BALLS

My parents had always instilled in us the maxim: if a great opportunity presents itself, take it! Such an opportunity occurred when Pan Am announced plans to open a flight service crew base in Boston, Massachusetts, in the spring of 1980. This was a twofold bonus for me in that I upgraded my flying status to purser, as well as being able to live in one of the most historic and beautiful cities in America. Happily I would also be re-united with Elaine White, a dear friend whom I had not seen since training school, and the vivacious infamous Brenda Bagsley, *Miss B*, whom I had last seen bouncing her breasts in a Tokyo earthquake. I was moving up in the ranks at work, relocating to a fantastic city and reconnecting with great friends; life was grand!

Shortly after arriving in *Bean-town*, I moved into a sun-filled carriage house attached to an incredible brown-stone four-story house in Louisburg Square in historic Beacon Hill. In those days, rents there were considerably cheaper than could be found in Manhattan and I was able to live on my own without roommates for the first time in my life! The purser position came with a considerable raise in pay and I indulged myself with decorating my large, one-bedroom, sun-filled apartment with rustic pieces I found scouring the markets on weekends. I experienced a veritable sense of satisfaction whenever I returned from a trip and turned the key to my new home.

The Boston base was quite small, only 200 F/As or so in total and we were all within the same age-range, early 20s to 30s. Consequently we bonded quite quickly and rapidly became an extended family of sorts. Because everyone knew one another, on flights together we were relaxed and convivial and our layovers took on a party atmosphere. I have fond memories of rowdy picnics along the banks of the Charles River; champagne brunches while enjoying the Boston Pops Orchestra; exploring all of New England's many glorious destinations and Saturday softball games with the eponymous Boston Blue Balls, our pun on the famous Pan Am global logo. Martha's Vineyard, Nantucket and Provincetown on Cape Cod were frequent weekend destinations.

By far the easiest trip out of Boston was the run to San Juan, Puerto Rico. Not only was it a short flight in duration (under five hours), but the 48-hour layover was at the Dorado Hotel, a luxury hotel which contained a five star restaurant on the premises, where we could partake of gourmet meals courtesy of Pan Am! The fear of becoming poster-children for gluttony was never far from our minds, but I have to confess that after several trips to San Juan I developed quite a fondness for escargot and lobster thermidor, followed by a dessert of profiteroles. Since we had such a lengthy layover, we invariably ended up dancing the night away in one of the many night-clubs located in Old San Juan.

One San Juan layover is indelibly imprinted in my memory. I had been flying all month with *Miss B* and on the last trip of the month she thought it might be great fun if we spent the first day and night of our 48-hour Puerto Rico layover in the Bahamas gambling in the casinos in Nassau and doing some serious duty-free shopping before heading back to San Juan and home to Boston.

We purchased our inter-line discounted tickets to Nassau and boarded our little island-hopping commuter plane for the short trip over to the Bahamas. Everything went as planned. We checked into a hotel for the night, dressed to the nines and headed out for an evening of serious drinking and gambling. While I am not lucky at either cards or the roulette wheel (I find it hard to win an argument let alone money!), *Miss B* "cleaned up" with considerable success at both venues. The next day we passed a leisurely afternoon spending her earnings purchasing luxury goods and alcohol before strolling back to the airport for our flight to San Juan. We had given ourselves more than ample time to make our early-evening flight back and were not overly concerned when upon checking in for our flight we discovered that it was delayed due to inclement weather. What had started out as a slight summer gale had in fact escalated to a contender for storm of the century with gale forces winds and blackened skies illuminated by lightning and attended by ear-splitting booms of thunder. Thunderstorms are quite common in the Caribbean during the summer months and as we still had 24 hours to make our check-in for the return trip to Boston, we were not overly concerned. Sure enough, after a 45-minute weather delay, we boarded the small Cessna plane along with half a dozen other passengers for the short trip back to San Juan.

We were no sooner airborne than the skies darkened once again and we were in the midst of a maelstrom, the small aircraft tossed about like a tiny toy plane. Not only were we shaken violently from side to side like maracas but the plane lost altitude dropping hundreds of feet at the same time as we were pitched about in the cabin like rag-dolls. Just when we thought the worst turbulence had passed we were hurled into another precipitous descent. This lasted about 10 to 15 minutes or so but to the terrified occupants of that sardine box-sized cabin it was a life-time. Even though both *Miss B* and I were *safety professionals* and should have been cool, calm and collected, we soon joined in the screams, shouts and prayers for "Jesus to save us!" How ironic that we should meet our end on this tiny puddle-jumper when we daily worked on the 747, the behemoth of all aircraft!

When we finally wobbled from storm-tossed skies and landed, bouncing twice before limping to a stop, we all shouted "Halleluiah!" and praised Jesus before tumbling out of our would-be death trap as quickly as we could manage. *Miss B* and I both fell to the ground, kissed it and vowed never to get on anything smaller than an aircraft carrier, if we weren't being paid to fly on it!

CHAPTER 14

DRACULA'S CASTLE

Charter flights were also a staple of the Boston base and we often had the opportunity of flying into destinations not on Pan Am's regular route structure. One time, Elaine W and I were among a group of F/As working a trip to Romania and our layover was to be near the infamous castle of Vlad the Impala, the notorious 15th century prince who was the model for Bram Stoker's Count Dracula.

We were all excited to have garnered this trip and since we had 48 hours to explore the sights we decided to tour Bran Castle, Vlad's ancestral home. As luck would have it we arrived at our layover destination at dusk and checked into a quaint Romanian hotel which, in keeping with its major tourist attraction, resembled a hostelry from the 15th century. The exterior was white washed plaster and had thick timber supports and leaded latticed widows which opened on to the cobble-stoned square.

Even though the rooms contained every modern convenience; a television set, a mini-bar and a wall safe, what immediately caught my attention was the woven braid of garlic hanging over my window. My immediate thought was that this was a either a decorative device … or a local talisman to ward off evil. After congregating at the hotel bar and finding each of us had a braid of garlic at the window we laughingly decided that it was the perfect accoutrement for a hotel straight out of a Hollywood movie set. That night we wined and dined ourselves into oblivion at a delightful local establishment and on disbanding, made plans to tour the castle the next day. Not being overly superstitious but well versed in vampire lore, I nonetheless made certain the lock was secure on my latticed window and the garlic visible when I fell into a drunken slumber.

The night passed without incident and as planned we climbed out of the valley where our charming hotel was located and found the queue of tourists for Bran's Castle. The castle was an elaborate 15th

century fortress with the obligatory turrets, vast drafty halls and perfectly restored living quarters. What really was the showpiece to Vlad's chamber of horrors was the impressive causeway to the castle itself. It was here, as our guide dressed in a costume of Vlad's period dramatically informed us, that the Prince had impaled the heads of his vanquished enemies on spikes, supposedly hundreds at a time, earning him the sobriquet of Vlad the Impaler. I cannot recall the rest of the spiel, but I do recall that in the gloom of the late afternoon it wasn't hard to imagine the gruesome sight of decapitated heads grimacing in rictus lining the causeway up to the moat. Of course, being the modern sophisticated world travelers we were our crew laughed the tale off and proceeded to drink the night away when we returned to town. Once again, I fell exhausted into my quilt-covered bed.

Perhaps it was the local wine, or the figment of an over-imaginative mind, but around 3am I was startled awake by the baying of wild dogs, which immediately became wolves in my mind, howling in the woods adjacent to the hotel! Chortling at my own foolishness, I pulled the covers over my head and attempted to go back to sleep when the noise stopped. Perhaps half an hour passed before the howling started up again and shivering, I decided to peek out the window to see what was causing the commotion.

The sliver of a pale moon was no help in discerning if anything was amiss, but just to be on the safe side (I told myself), I made certain that the garlic braid still graced my window and placed a chair against the door handle for good measure. I finally fell into a fitful slumber and sheepishly shared my creepy night's tale with my crew when we gathered in the lobby the next morning to check out and return to the airport. There was no argument.

Oddly enough, we had all been awakened in the night and we shared similar stories of being nearly frightened out of our wits. In the light of day we could laugh at the conclusion that our dramatic tour guide had probably been successful in implanting fear of Dracula in our subconscious mindsets, but we decided that it was good to be returning home to Boston, where, as far as we knew, vampires did not prowl the night.

CHAPTER 15

WARSAW, POLAND

Chicago, Illinois, had a huge Polish emigrant population and as a consequence Pan Am regularly operated charters between the bustling US metropolis to Dansk and Krakow. One of my less than stellar moments occurred while on a layover in Krakow.

It was an unusually hot summer that year and Chicago was literally sweltering. Our Boston-based crew had flown into town to work a charter transporting an eminent Polish ballet troop from Chicago back home to Warsaw. We had 24 hours to party in Chi-town before departing for Poland so we hit the streets running, aiming to squeeze in as many nightclubs as possible before assuming flight duties the next day.

To our delight, the dance company who had charted the flight was composed of artists mostly in their late 20s or early 30s, eager to chaperone us once we'd reached their hometown. Due to the fame of our ebullient hosts, we were treated like rock stars and given carte-blanche to the city's best restaurants and nightspots. What would have been in normal circumstance a fantastic 72-hour layover in one of Europe's most storied and charming cities turned into a visit most diplomats would envy.

At each of the city's monuments, museums and cathedrals we were given private tours and allowed access to spots few tourists ever encounter or get a chance to visit. We were given guided tours of the home of Chopin, Poland's most famous composer, and spent our nights partying in the Praga district. I will never forget a champagne picnic our hosts provided for us in the beautiful Royal Lazienki Park; not only for the abundance of delicious food, but the constant flow of delightful local wines.

But it was the night-life where our new-found friends truly excelled at showing us an incredible time. They escorted us from one glittering party to another. I have fond memories of dancing on tables with wild abandon and staggering back to the hotel fairly exhausted and falling thoroughly drunk into bed.

Our last night in Warsaw coincided with a celebration for St John's day. We were driven to a palatial home on the outskirts of town and given quite literally a feast. With a delicious five course meal, copious amounts of alcohol were consumed, in particular an orange-flavored liqueur, which, while seemingly mild and harmless, proved to give an amazingly potent punch. The soiree proceeded into the wee hours of the morning and as our hosts were now as thoroughly intoxicated as we were, we decided not to impose upon their hospitality and make our own way back into the city and the hotel. While waiting for a couple of taxis to hail we noticed a train headed for the city just in front of us. Although spectacularly drunk, we decided it would be a great adventure to experience public transportation on our last night/early morning in town.

Even at this ungodly hour the train was packed with passengers, but in our gregarious state we crammed ourselves into the already full-to-capacity crowd. Unfortunately for me this was one of the hottest nights of the summer and the lurching movement of the train, coupled with the poignant odor of sweat-drenched citizenry packed like sardines in the confines of the train cabin proved to be too much for an increasingly distressed stomach.

I was holding onto the straps of a plastic handle, being tossed about like a rag-doll by the train, when the urge to vomit became an over-whelming desire. Gagging and desperately attempting to keep the contents of our night's revelry in my stomach and not over my fellow travelers, my eyes bugged in alarm at my predicament. I was literally trapped in the middle of a crowded lurching train. My mouth was covered with my free hand and my sense of smell was over-whelmed by what can only be politely described as unwashed humanity. As I was jostled by the crowd I wildly tried to reach a window, which was inexplicably, considering the heat of the night, totally closed.

Suddenly, the oppressive confines of the lurching train became too much for my stomach to handle and in a blind panic I spotted the large handbag of Maria, one of the crew members who were staggering right next to me. Lifting the flap, I heaved the contents of the night's debauchery into her bag, eliciting a scream of shock from Marie and the scrambled movement from the crowd. Fortunately for me two things occurred at once: I passed out and we reached our stop, a short distance from the hotel. I awoke hours later, undressed and face down on the cold floor of the bathroom in my hotel room.

The following morning, after I had packed my bags, dressed and boarded the crew bus for the trip to the airport, mortified by my actions of the previous evening, I made attempts to placate a furious Maria who loudly told me that she was grateful she only carried her make-up in that bag which I DEFINETLY would be replacing at the duty free shop at the Krakow airport!

We dead-headed to London and then back home to Boston, with Maria glaring at me continually until finally, half-way through the flight, she burst out laughing saying in retrospect that, "I was trapped between a rock and a hard place."

CHAPTER 16

VULGARIANS IN VENICE

In the same way as an awe-inspiring painting or a riveting film can, your first sight of a new destination can have an incredible impact on your memory. My initial sighting of Venice, the Renaissance jewel of a city, was at night. Approaching this majestic city of islands from the Adriatic Sea and seated in the bow of a Vaporetto (a water taxi), I was mesmerized by the view in front of us, a floating metropolis lit by millions of twinkling lights.

Countless paintings, films and photographs have depicted this historic view but nonetheless, that moment remains one of my fondest memories.

After an uneventful flight from Boston, all fatigue was forgotten, banished the moment we docked at the picturesque palazzo which was to be our home for the next 72 hours. The gods of fortune were certainly in our favor as our lay-over coincided with the start of Carnevale (occurring during the month of February) and the entire city was transformed into a Renaissance fantasy, with every structure beautifully lit and Venetians everywhere bedecked in elegant costumes and masks.

With a few hurried purchases under our belts, we quickly joined the throngs celebrating the night away. On a recent forage through stored items in my attic, I found the ankle-length, black-wool crepe hooded cape and gilt and feathered mask I bought that night! I vaguely recall watching the sunrise over Piazza San Marco, mystified and grateful that none of us had taken a drunken tumble into a canal!

Having waxed poetically about my first visual impression of Venice by the gloss of a Carnevale-lit background, I must state that the harsh light of day presented a totally different façade. Venice, as charming and architecturally unique as any place on earth, in the cold sobriety of sunlight resembled nothing so much as an ageing courtesan; one whose pan-caked, heavily applied make-up, could not quite disguise the ravages of time. In addition to the alarming rate that the Adriatic Sea was reclaiming the city, the smell of the sewage and flotsam bobbing in the canals was overwhelming. In hindsight, there must have been some sixth sense of preservation that had prevented our group of drunken revelers from tumbling into the dark waters throughout the city. I have to admit that even though I hadn't really given much thought to or thoroughly considered the mechanics of the sanitation/sewerage involved in a floating city; lack of sobriety does have its advantages at times.

After the night's debaucheries, we rented a gondola and set about touring Venice in earnest via its series of canals. During the course of the next two days we explored the Piazza San Marco, admiring the architecture of St Mark's Basilica and taking time out to feed the multitude of pigeons, which treated the place as their personal roost. We managed to take in all of the major tourist destinations, marveling at the Doges Palace, once the center of Venetian society, and passing beneath the Bridge of Sighs and the magnificent Rialto Bridge, before refueling at Harry's Bar where we consumed copious amounts of Bellinis.

It's fair to state that every country has its portion of loud-mouthed, uncouth and unrefined citizens, who, when abroad, present their respective nations in the worst possible light. Add to that mixture of boorish behavior, a sartorial sense that is sadly lacking in either taste or style and you have all the elements of a classic cultural disaster.

I confronted the specter of the ugly American tourist when I visited Murano Island, a place long-held in esteem for its hand-blown glassware and works of art. After touring the facilities I purchased a beautifully sculpted glass shell as a wedding present and was admiring the craftsmanship and skill involved in creating these masterpieces, when the proverbial bull entered the china shop.

The bovine analogy was well suited as the couple who stomped through the entryway resembled the prize-winning entry in a country fair; a buxom, over-fed heifer accompanied by her snorting, red-faced bull of a consort. Her hair, which was a color red not found in nature, was piled atop her head in a bee-hive lacquered in place with at least two cans of aqua-net, a hair spray popular in the '60s; her outlandish figure was literally squeezed into a lurid floral-print dress that only served to accentuate her battle-ship bosom and pre-ponderous derriere; and rhinestone cats-eye sunglasses and bright pink lip-stick only added to the shock value of an extremely large woman tottering on sling-back kitten-heeled sandals.

Her crimson-faced husband, equally rotund, was sporting a lime-green polyester leisure-suit with a white belt which made a vain attempt to gird the massive belly protruding over his spindly legs. His outfit was accessorized with thick soled, sensible shoes with white socks. Their only concessions to the weather in Venice were matching bright yellow rain-coasts, which gave them both the appearance of over-aged, overweight, school-crossing guards. Both were well over 6ft and looked like towering giants in search of a snack.

I'm not sure who recovered first from the sight of this garish couple (I know that my mouth was open in shock), but the stylishly dressed Italian sales lady approached them (although with trepidation) and after wishing them *buona sera*, asked if she could be of any assistance.

Whether out of sheer rudeness or the fact that the clerk wasn't visible beneath her bountiful bosom, the wife boomed out in a voice like a fog-horn in an unmistakable American twang, "MY GAWD HERMAN, WOULD YA LOOK AT ALL THESE GAUDY TRINKETS". I was thinking to myself, "OHH REALLY?? ...Talk about calling the kettle 'beige'".... when her left ham-sized buttock bumped against a counter-top sending several pieces shattering to the ground.

Both the sales lady and myself were aghast. But before any further conversation could ensue, the manager, frowning and furious, exploded from his office and approached the obese, obtuse couple, informing them in a manner that would brook no further discussion that they were responsible for and would have to pay for the damage they had caused.

The brouhaha had reached a lively crescendo when I collected my parcel and headed for the door. As I left I glanced back just in time to see the now beet-red-faced husband glaring at the store manager as he handed over his American Express card.

As I stepped into the street, I couldn't wipe a huge smile from my face, happy in the extreme that karma was doled out in equal measure, to the kind and deserving as well as to the crass.

CHAPTER 17

SUIT OF LIGHTS

I have never been enamoured of blood sports, particularly where it involves the senseless death of an animal. However after much badgering by my crew, I begrudgingly consented to attend a bullfight in Seville, Spain.

Late one afternoon, I found myself entering the Plaza de Torres. Despite my misgivings, in Spain and in Seville in particular, a bullfight is considered an art form and is awarded the same status as the opera in Italy or a baseball game in America. What prevented the afternoon from being a complete waste for me was the grand spectacle, the theatrics evoked to whip the spectators into a frenzy. I have to admit the crowd was a spectacle in itself!

It is difficult to associate the slaughter of a maddened bull with a fashion show, but everyone in attendance was literally dressed to impress. High society was in full display in the latest style of the day. I could just as easily have imagined myself in the front row at Balenciaga's Fall Collection fashion show as in a bullring!

First the crowd applauded a procession of brightly dressed matadors wearing pointed hats, riding on horseback and carrying lances decorated in ribbons. Next the crowd applauded the Banderillos, the bull fighters on foot clad in canary yellow, who would use their be-ribboned spear-like-sticks to puncture the bull's neck muscles. Seeing as how the poor bull was out-numbered more than five to one, I was less than impressed and my empathy lay decidedly with the bull. I had already mapped out my escape from the stands when the crowd erupted in a thunderous roar of appreciation heralding the grand entrance of El Matador! This then, was the main event.

Sitting back down, I had to admit that all things considered he cut quite an impressive figure in an emerald green silk sequined and embroidered short fitted jacket and knee breeches, white silk stockings and black leather pumps. He was wearing a flat topped hat with a round bulb above each ear (a montera), rakishly cocked in his brilliantly pomaded hair. And the piece de resistance was a magenta cape dramatically draped across his shoulders.

His outfit would have made Liberace, a flamboyant Las Vegas entertainer known for his outrageous costumes, green with envy, and his pants while literally a second skin they were so tight, would have given him apoplexy! I remember thinking to myself that on the off chance that I had to face a horned beast that was not only angry but weighed a ton or more and had every intention of either maiming or killing you, you might as well go out in style!

The action that ensued was as choreographed as any ballet. With each pass of the bull, the matador would pivot gracefully just out of reach of the bull's horns, flaunting the red cape with a flourish worthy of a flamenco dancer. At each pass of the cape, the bull's horns seemingly missing the matador by centimetres, the crowd roared its approval with full throated shouts of, "OLE"!

I however was routing for the bull and envisioned a scenario whereby the matador's tightly packed breeches were caught on the tip of the bull's horn smack in the middle of his derriere and he was thrown spectacularly (unhurt of course) into the crowd!

Unfortunately, my fantasy scenario was not to be, and after suffering horrendous thrusts and stabs by the picadors, the beast was brought down by several thrusts from the matador's blade. Then as now, I could not find it in me to find any redeeming value in this so-called sport and voiced my disgust vociferously to anyone within hearing distance, a fact that made me a social pariah in the section where I was seated.

As for my crew-members, we were unanimous in our assessment of the carnage we had just witnessed, a barbaric event that none of us wished to experience again. I'd like to think that the germination of the idea that launched PETA (People for the Ethical Treatment of

Animals) was born that afternoon, the only positive thing that resulted from a horrific spectacle.

Thankfully, that afternoon spent in the Plaza de Toros was not our ultimate experience in Spain. Our crew was scheduled to ferry the aircraft back to Boston, a procedure whereby an aircraft was flown back empty of passengers (excepting the crew of course) for positioning for another route. Since we had quite a while before our next scheduled working flight, a group of us decided to spend our remaining time in Spain exploring its famous castles. Utilizing our airline discounts and renting cars we set out on a tour of Spain worthy of Don Quixote! After consulting guide books we decided on four destinations, the memories of which permeate my more pleasant dreams to this day.

First up on our caravan of castles was the Alcazar de Segovia, which was a Disney fantasy brought to life. Besides being spectacularly beautiful, it is steeped in history being the first place where Queen Isabel and King Ferdinand (who funded Columbus expeditions to the New World) met. I also like to think that we were in the vanguard of young hip Americans who had discovered just how delightful the wines of Spain were as we explored the vineyards and restaurants of Spain.

Next up was the Castle Olite, an incredibly beautiful edifice located in Navarre, where we frequented excellent restaurants and the Ochoa winery, which was situated near yet another spectacular wine region of Rioja. We toured the Mota, which served as a royal residence and later as a prison, before its current reincarnation as an art gallery. But far and away the culmination of our grand tour, and my favourite castle in Spain, was the Alhambra, situated in Granada. This majestic masterpiece was built by the Moors (Muslims from North Africa) in the 13th Century. Alhambra is the Spanish rendering of the Arabic word for red-castle, a fact no-doubt derived from the dusty-red stone that was used to construct the fortress-like walls surrounding the castle.

Hollywood could not have improved upon the spectacular site, as we arrived just before sunset, mouths agape at the gorgeous view of the castle, sitting on a hilltop called La Sabika, surrounded by a forest of Cypress trees.

The most glorious section of the castle was the Palacio Nazaries, the residential quarters, which were entered after passing magnificent courtyards containing reflecting pools that were filled with water lilies, all leading to the most impressive and beautiful rooms of all. My senses were over-whelmed when I entered the main chambers, which were filled on every wall and ceiling with intricate geometric carvings and tiling said to be an expression of the beauty of the universe. My mind was still taking in these wonders when we reluctantly exited the castle through the exquisite Parlial gardens.

The next day, seated in a window seat on an Iberia (Spain's national airline) flight headed back to Boston and home, I dreamed of being Don Quixote, and my magnificent quest of the castles of Spain.

CHAPTER 18

PORTUGAL

Another of my enduring memories is of layovers in Lisbon and Estoril, Portugal. Whenever I was in either city I felt transported to a grander era before WWII, one in which louche royalty, arms dealers, fading movie stars and millionaires of dubious backgrounds rubbed shoulders with high-stakes gamblers in some of the most glamorous casinos in Europe. The beaches in both places were a sun-worshipper's paradise and surfers flocked especially to the beaches of Tameriz, famous for its breaks.

We were lucky enough to layover at Estoril's famous Hotel Palacio, which was the basis for Ian Fleming's *Casino Royale* from the James Bond series of novels (and later films). Even though the hotel had seen better days by the late '70s it was still magnificent and it was quite easy to envision dashing tuxedo-clad men and be-jewelled women in diaphanous gowns strolling through the lobby on their way to either win or lose fortunes in its famous casino.

From the mosaic-paved promenade in front of the hotel you could enjoy a leisurely hike to nearby Cascais and dine in some the best cafes and watering holes in Europe. My absolute favourite meal was had in a small seaside *boite* facing the sea, dining on the best paella I have ever tasted, either now or then!

In Lisbon, we were lucky enough to spend time touring the Jeronimos Monastery, the final resting place of explorer Vasco da Games and a magnificent church whose cloisters are considered the most beautiful in the world, and which is in fact listed as a World Heritage site.

Another spectacular spot was the Belem Tower, a watchtower that was built in the 1500s and which is also another World Heritage site. Given my affinity for castles and medieval architecture, I always looked forward to exploring St George's Castle, with its bird's eye view of the city, its grounds surrounded by roaming peacocks.

We never failed to stroll through the Parque Das Nacoes, the 21st century district that was a stark contrast to the surrounding neighbourhoods and older sections of the city. I believe that we single-handedly kept the economy of Portugal in the green by the amount of money we spent inhabiting the bars, shops and restaurants of that area.

One of my favourite wines at that time was Mateus, which I bought frequently along with home-made tiles and gorgeous tapestries. I would regularly lug a wooden crate of the wine through customs, onto the plane and back to Boston with me.

Unfortunately, after my last layover in Lisbon, having carefully carted a heavy-wooden crate filled with wine safely through all those obstacles, I dropped it while removing it from the trunk of my car in front of my house, shattering all 12 bottles, all the while howling obscenities as my precious wine poured on to the cobbled streets.

Little did I know that the winds of change were blowing in the form of an oil embargo that would directly affect American air carriers, and particularly the junior F/As, those of us with the least seniority.

The oil embargo forced layoffs of those at the bottom of the ranks and the closure of Pan Am's FA base in Boston, bringing my time in Massachusetts to an end.

CHAPTER 19

LONDON CALLING

The old adage goes that as one door closes another opens to a new direction and new opportunities. The oil embargo brought about changes in every F/A's life, none more so than in the lives of those of us based in Boston, who were faced with the hard choice of being furloughed with the prospect of not being recalled to duty (and a job), or making a major change in our lives by relocating to another city. If we opted to remain active employees we were given the choice of two cities that were expanding their F/A's base, Honolulu, Hawaii or London, England. Given that most people would give their eye-teeth to visit let alone live in either city, it seemed a ludicrously luxurious choice to make, made even sweeter by the fact that Pan Am was paying to move all our essential belongings with us.

After much soul-searching I reasoned that although living in a tropical paradise had outstanding benefits I had never lived outside of the US and the cultural riches and the lure of living in London were undeniable.

Within a few weeks, I had packed up my apartment and stored my furniture and most of my worldly possessions. Then, after packing the essentials for a new life in England, I bid a tearful good-bye to Boston and assuming my best attempt at a stiff upper lip, headed to London and a new chapter of my life.

Filled with the confidence that only youth and foolishness can provide, I arrived in London eager to take Europe by storm. I was mistakenly filled with the notion that in my mid-20s I was quite the sophisticate and was well equipped to deal with any situation with a cool and level head.

My un-worldliness and naivety were about to prove me wrong.

Pan Am had provided a hotel for us in central London until we found accommodation of our own. It was my second day in the city and I was somewhat bewilderedly wandering around a crowded Piccadilly Circus, city map in hand, when I bumped into two seemingly helpful gentlemen, who offered first their apologies and then enquired if I needed assistance.

Grateful for their kindly gesture, I asked them if they knew the way to the Pan Am ticket office which was located not too far away. Unfortunately, however, when they opened their mouths to give me directions, I found I could not understand a single word of their thick cockney accents. Even though I assumed it was English they were speaking I was at a complete loss to know what they had just said. From the blank and vapid expression on my face I gathered they also knew that I didn't quite grasp what they had said, so I went with them willingly when they politely grabbed me by my arms and escorted me across the street pointing me to the Pan Am ticket office a few meters down the road.

Smiling and thanking them for their assistance, I carried on down the road thinking to myself how kind and thoughtful the citizens of London were. It was not until I reached the ticket office and fumbled through every pocket of my trench coat that it dawned on me that my helpful strangers had relieved me not only of my wallet but of a wad of American Express Travelers' checks as well. I stood in the center of the office floor dumbfounded with the awful realization that every dime I had had been *lifted* from me like a country bumpkin on his first foray into the city. Near to tears, I was filled with first anger and then anxiety when the Pam Am agent working the counter took pity on me and generously gave me enough cash to catch a taxi back to my hotel.

Later when I made a report to the London Metropolitan Police I found out that the two had been preying on unsuspecting tourists for weeks. I was ready to crawl into a ball of misery and was feeling quite sorry for myself when I remembered that my mother had suggested that I keep my passport and the receipts of my travelers' checks together, in the hotel safe! Sure enough that afternoon in the American Express office I was not only able to report that the checks were stolen but was also immediately reissued a new allotment of checks covering my losses. I was without my wallet and my Boston identification, both of which could be replaced, but I still had my US passport and Pan Am ID.

The upshot to this whole situation was that I had learned a hard but valuable lesson; ALWAYS keep your eyes on the hand that is offered to you because the other one might very well be deep in your pocket!

Moments before being *helped*.

CHAPTER 20

THE JA-JA GIRLS

During my first few weeks of flying out of London, I could have been forgiven for assuming that Pan Am was, in actuality, a subsidiary of SAS; Scandinavian Airlines System, due to the fact that the majority of all the F/As based there were either Swedish, Norwegian, Danish or Finnish. There was a smattering of other European nations represented including England, France and Germany, but London-Heathrow was the stronghold of Nordic Goddesses.

The most common names of my flying partners were Inga-Britt, Mae-Britt, Gisella, Olga, Ana-Lisa, Helga or Heidi, with nary a Mary or Jane amongst them!

Pan Am's reputation as a first-class airline was well deserved, in no small part due to its London-based Nordic contention. These women had honed skills garnered from years working the First Class cabin into an art form that they also utilized in their own homes. I can vividly recall the many soirees and dazzling dinner parties that were presided over by these ladies, in homes and flats that were immaculately decorated.

In an era in which beautiful women were paramount to an airlines reputation (and Pan Am was indeed famous for its gorgeous F/As), the London base represented the absolute cream of the crop! I had never seen so many strikingly tall, blonde and glamorous women in my life. In fact, Pan Am had hired more than its share of former Miss World and Miss Universe contestants; ladies who had proudly worn the crowns of their representative nations. Every event, every occasion was a fashion parade and these ladies did their utmost to present themselves in the best possible manner.

Immaculately coiffed and made up, they never ceased to draw admiring glances as they strolled through the corridors of Heathrow airport on their way to yet another glamorous destination.

As well as always being immaculately groomed, the London based girls were invariably bedecked in jewels, the most common Pan Am uniform accessory being a strand of gleaming pearls, embellished by other glittering gems they had acquired in their jaunts around the world.

On Pan Am's round the world flights flight 1 and 2, crews would congregate in New Delhi and I can still hear the titters of derisive laughter as the Ja-Ja girls spotted the LAX crews making their way across the tarmac, "Schatze look – ze LA girls are wearing Bonne-Belle make-up. How dreadful!"

Ja-Ja girls.

Even though they worked for an American carrier, either in a group or chatting amongst themselves on the plane, they hardly ever spoke English. I spent countless hours amusing myself observing the inflight conversations during our down-time in the galleys when, in describing some juicy tit-bit of jump-seat gossip to one another, they might use only one word of English in any given sentence. However, it wasn't difficult to garner the gist of the conversation by observing the theatrical facial expressions and gestures of the participants.

Any given layover indiscretion was fair-game and fodder for inflight analysis; and while I didn't understand half of what was being said, I still burst out laughing when I recall our blonde beauties; heads huddled together in the galley, rehashing the latest domestic drama or layover infidelity.

For example,

Swedish: Astrid – "Jag horde att Freja hon vor gravid!!" (I heard that Freja was pregnant!!). At which point, Inga-Britt dropped her nail file in horror and shouted, "Stanna!! Herre Gud!!" (Stop!! Good God!!).

Norwegian: Ingrid to Mathilde – "Er hun dating en rik man?" (Is she dating a wealthy man?) To which Mathilde replied with a smug look on her face, "Jeg horte at hun var elskerinnen til statsministerien!" (Oh no girl ... I heard that she was the mistress of the Prime Minister!)

Dannish: Maja leaning in conspiratorially to Sige who was busy re-applying her lip-stick – "Ile kobte nende masser at pelsfrakker og sarykker!!" (He brought her lots of fur coats and jewellery!)

To simplify things and since verbally it sounded that way to me, I affectionately referred to all of my lovely Nordic ladies as the *Ja-Ja* girls!

Pan Am's Scandinavian F/As were not solely defined by their beauty. These were not frivolous women by any means. Each and every one these ladies was not only a well-educated sophisticate, but also an astute negotiator. Any one of them could use their innate charm to out-manoeuvre and out-bargain the most cunning merchant in the world.

I must confess that I had never paid attention to fine china, crystal or silverware before I was tutored in the finer points of luxury goods by these gracious ladies. A typical layover in France would involve one of the girls purring, "Come darling, ve are going to the Limoges (or Baccarat or Lalique) factory. You must purchase something nice for your flat!" Or, if I happened to be in Germany, I might hear, "Mach schnell Liebling, ve are going to the Rosenthal factory; every man should have descent china." Thanks to these patient ladies, I acquired not only quite a few *nice things for my flat*, but a more refined sense of the parameters of style and life's finer pleasures.

These ladies could spot a flaw in a gem-stone in the jewellery markets of Beirut or New Delhi without the aid of a jeweller's loupe. They could expertly appraise the quality and value of any gem with the skill of a master jeweller.

I learnt much about choosing an authentic Persian carpet or a runner in Istanbul just from observing these ladies in their element, heatedly bargaining and succeeding in getting the best deal possible. They taught me how to discern the finest quality caviar in Tehran, how to order the freshest seafood from the Bosporus in Istanbul and where to find the tastiest curry in New Delhi.

Thanks to their tutelage, I became as adept as any of them at choosing the finest quality and bargaining for the best deals possible on several continents. I could not have asked for better teachers and I am forever in their debt.

For all the kindness, compassion, patience and guidance but most importantly, for all the life-long friendship that were forged, I'd like to give a heartfelt thank you to all of my Ja-Ja Goddesses!

Swedish: Tack sa mycket!

German: Schoenen Dank!

Norwegian: Takk sa mye!

Finnish: Kiitos paljon!

Danish: Takk sa meget!

CHAPTER 21

LOST IN TRANSLATION

English, or a form thereof, is a language spoken by 1.8 billion people worldwide. Whether or not we actually understand each other or express our intentions to one another correctly, is a matter open to debate. This was never more evident than on a night-time flight from London to New Delhi, India.

The time that members of the cabin take their meals breaks, or commiserate with one another about the demanding and difficult passengers on the flight, usually occurs after the meal has been served and during screening of the inflight movie.

While leaving the galley area where this particular crew was relaxing (okay, gossiping and swapping plans for our layover and swapping shopping tips for the bazaars of New Delhi), I came across a thoroughly disgruntled Indian gentleman muttering curses in what I gathered was Hindi and looking thunderously from beneath his turban at me as I came into view. Stopping to ask what the problem was I was met with a furious splutter, "I have been FINGERING the hostess for over an hour and STILL she has not COME!!!" After biting the inside of my mouth and regaining my composure I asked what he required of the hostess and re-set his call button, the object that he had been *fingering*.

I barely made it through the galley curtains before bursting into raucous and uncontrollable laughter! When I could breathe I explained what had happened, adding, "I knew you bitches were supposed to be COLD but I had no idea that it took an hour of FINGERING to get your attention or to get you to COME!"

For the remainder of the flight, each of the cold-hearted, exotic beauties made it a point to give the gentleman in seat 32C her warmest, most come-hither smile and her undivided attention, hopefully putting the *Ice Maiden* sobriquet to rest for at least on

THIS flight!

New Delhi, India

CHAPTER 22

THE THREE AMIGOS

Whenever I recall the years I spent based in the UK, I can't help but reminisce on the life-long friendships that were forged there. Two people in particular will always hold a special place in my heart: Jane Horwell and Konrad Bajan.

Jane was a petite and vivacious blonde from Colorado, whose pixie-style haircut gave her an amazing resemblance to Mia Farrow (circa *Rosemary's Baby*). Konrad was a strapping, strikingly handsome black haired, blue-eyed South African, whose impeccable hearing always brought to mind a member of the diplomatic corps, which in a sense, as a representative of Pan Am World Airways, he was!

I first crossed paths with these two at one of the numerous social gatherings that the London-Heathrow based F/As were renowned for. This blonde beauty and the dashing dark haired man were the centre of attention, everyone drifting into their orbit. Jane had her head thrown back in raucous laughter at some off-color remark or joke that Konrad was whispering to her and I remember thinking that these two, were two of the most attractive and glamorous people that I had ever laid eyes on. When Konrad, with a joint in his mouth and a devilish glean in his eyes invited me to join them, I crossed the room without hesitation and was welcomed into their inner sanctum.

From that day on we were pretty much inseparable, bidding to fly together whenever possible and spending our days off carousing in the many nightclubs and upscale venues of London, earning the sobriquet of *The Three Amigos*. Annabelle's, Heaven and Ronnie Scott's Jazz Club were favourite haunts. While both Jane and I lived in central London, Jane in South Kensington and myself in Kensington proper, just behind the old Biba's Emporium on Kensington High St, we spent most of our days off at Konrad's considerably more palatial digs outside the city.

Konrad was fortunate enough to live in a well-manicured and exquisitely furnished cottage in Windsor, which was conveniently located next door to Elton John's estate and bordered the grounds of Windsor Castle. Consequently his abode was the centre of most of our social gatherings. With Elton John as his closest neighbour, and his place set on acres of land abutting the forested grounds of Windsor Castle, loud and raucous parties were held Chez Konrad with regularity, with no fear of disturbing the neighbours!

Jane was the most intellectual and sensible member of the group and took pleasure in organizing outings of a more cultural nature, such as visits to Edinburgh Castle, Brighton and Stonehenge. Thanks to her intervention, we were able to learn about and experience some of the historical sites of Great Britain into our itinerary to counter-balance our pub-crawls and frantic nightclubbing. Flying with either of them was a delight and if mischief was on the horizon we unerringly found ourselves involved, either directly or indirectly, smack dab in the middle.

Konrad had a totally irreverent sense of humour and everything and everyone within his radius was considered fair game. Konrad's most notorious and hilarious escapade took place while we were working the business class cabin from London to Tehran.

A stern faced and extremely imperious eastern woman, who was obviously used to her every whim being catered to by her servants, waved her hand dismissively at Konrad as he was passing through the cabin. After pointing to the toddler seated next to her, she haughtily demanded that Konrad, "change my baby." Standing nearby and eyes widening in indignation, I was just about to point out we were neither nannies nor nurses when with a smirk on his face, Konrad winked at me and proceeded to approach a couple travelling a few rows behind the *pampered princess* who had a tussled-headed blonde child about the same age as the sodden-diapered off-spring of the obnoxious woman.

Upon receiving permission from the parents of the obviously European couple to "take a stroll with their child", Konrad, with the blonde baby held aloft, icily approached the Iranian woman and in a tone of voice that would not have been out of place in Buckingham Palace said, "Madam, would this child do? It is quite the best I could manage at such short notice; however... it IS a change!"

Unable to contain myself, I doubled over with laughter which was shared by everyone else within hearing distance. Her eyes narrowing and with her nose up-turned, the woman snatched up her own child and stormed off in a huff to change her own baby's diaper.

Keep in mind this incident occurred in the dark ages, before either political correctness or cell phones were in existence. If this incident had have occurred today, I am certain that we would have both been taken to task for our cheeky response.

On another occasion, Konrad and I were working the liquor cart together on a flight from JFK to London-Heathrow. An extremely proper Englishman looked up from his Financial Times and enquired of me if we had "any fags on board". Remember this was during the "dark ages" and at that time, smoking was not only permitted on board flights, but was prevalent on every aircraft crossing the Atlantic.

In England and in a much more innocent age, the term *fag* referred to cigarettes. Without missing a beat, I leaned across the cart and in a quite audible stage whisper, I said to Konrad, "Would you mind stepping back in coach and tell Robert that there is a man here who would like a word with him?" Konrad guffawed and left the cart in some haste, while one prim and proper Englishman bristled with indignation.

The three Amigos!

CHAPTER 23

DAMSELS IN DISTRESS

My first impression of India is that we had crashed and I was now in some form of purgatory!

It was the middle of the monsoon season and we had arrived shortly before the break of dawn and the surrounding landscape had taken on an eerie, other world aspect, with red-coloured dust swirling in eddies around the crew bus and giving everything in sight a dreamlike appearance. Combined with the over-whelming heat and humidity, I could well imagine that I had somehow *crossed-over* into another realm of existence altogether.

Thankfully, a sense of reality was restored when we arrived at the Ashoka Palace Hotel. The sun was rising as we pulled into the driveway of one of the most beautiful hotels I had ever laid eyes on, a pink-hued sandstone edifice that was a marvel and quite a relief to behold.

I was once again flying with my dear friend Yvonne Scherer and after waking from a much-needed nap, Yvonne and I mapped out our plans for the layover.

First on our itinerary was a visit to the historic Red Fort, a former Moghul palace and the major land mark in New Delhi, for a spice infused lunch at its famous tea house. After refreshing our palates with Mango Lassis (a drink made from the fruit of a mango and yoghurt) we made our way to the Lahore Gate, a major bazaar, and got down to the serious business of shopping for gem-stones which were to be set into jewellery in Bangkok the next leg of our round-the-world excursion. We spent hours bargaining (successfully I might add) over the prices of brass and sandalwood trinkets to add to the treasure trove of items we had previously purchased in Beirut and Tehran.

By the time the heat of the late afternoon had set in, we were thoroughly exhausted. Hauling our newly acquired loot with us, we hailed a rickshaw bicycle back to the exquisite luxury of our air-conditioned rooms. After consuming several curried dishes and cocktails while dining poolside at the hotel, we decided to admire and catalogue the items from our day of shopping. At that time F/As were not allocated single rooms but had to share a double room with another crew member, the cock-pit crew and inflight purser being the exception to this archaic rule. As I was the only male F/A on this trip, even though I was by far the most junior F/A, I was given a spacious room all to myself, a fact that wasn't appreciated by some of the more *senior* ladies on the crew.

After spending more than two weeks working, shopping and partying together, Yvonne and I not only enjoyed each other's company, but had grown as close as siblings. Without hesitation, I invited her to share my double room and she happily accepted. We ordered yet another bottle of wine and spent hours making plans for the remainder of the trip. By this time we were both three-sheets to the wind and rapidly becoming thoroughly inebriated. The air conditioner was cranked up to full volume and we were dressed in long cotton night shirts that we had purchased earlier in the day. At some point Yvonne decided that we should undergo a *spa* treatment and she proceeded to concoct a mixture of avocado (which she had planned as having for lunch) and mayonnaise from her supply of condiments that she was never without. Yvonne was blessed with a luxurious mane of hair that she explained was the by-product of her *beauty treatments*. She convinced me to follow her example and by now we looked like crazy characters from a *I love Lucy* episode, our faces smeared with a green gunk and the avocado/mayo worked into our scalps, which we then covered with the plastic shower caps from the bathroom.

It must have been close to 3am and we were laughing hysterically at how ridiculous we looked, when an extremely loud brass gong was rung repeatedly in the hallway, obviously an alarm of some sort. By now, the night porters were banging on the doors of each room on the floor shouting, "Please to hurry to the fire escape!" Someone had started a fire in the waste bin on the floor below with a carelessly discarded cigarette. Since we were located on the 5th floor this gave me a severe bout of trepidation. Before we had a moment to consider out comical appearances we were ushered into the now teeming hallway and told that the elevator couldn't be used and that fire ladders were poised ready to help us descend to the safety of the ground below. I had opened my mouth to make a comment to Yvonne when I was grabbed by the elbow and ushered to the ladder by a kindly turbaned gentleman who shouted, "Madam, madam, this way madam, hurry!" I imagined that my hairy legs were covered not only by the darkness of the night but by my flowing night-shirt, so I didn't utter a word as both Yvonne and myself were hurriedly escorted down the ladder by a male member of the hotel staff.

When we finally reached the bottom rung of the ladder, we were gently led away from danger with intonations of, "Are you alright madam, not to worry madam, all is well." I was utterly mortified by my predicament but kept my mouth closed on the off chance that as just one of the *frail madams* that had been escorted to safety, I could melt into the crowd, Yvonne clutching my arm trying not to double over in laughter. All would have gone well except at that moment another member of our crew called out, "Where is Tal?" Yvonne and I looked at each other and fell to the ground, bent over with laughter, while she wiped some of the green glob from my face and shouted, "He's right here!"

Thankfully, this was well before the days of smart phones, digital cameras and, worst of all, the internet, otherwise I would have been a viral sensation, forever notorious for my late night ladder escapade! For the remainder of the trip, around-the-world snickers of *madam, madam, this way madam* followed me everywhere I went.

CHAPTER 24

DOWNHILL MADNESS

One of my more memorable holidays occurred in the mountains of Colorado while being accompanied by Jane and Konrad.

Jane had organised a week-long Christmas getaway in Vail, Colorado, where her family maintained a magnificent ski-chalet. Along with the gorgeous vistas of the awe-inspiring Rocky Mountains, her ski chalet was the perfect setting for sybaritic partying with numerous decks giving us a 360-degree view of the mountains and a hot tub that could easily accommodate 10 adults. As there were only three of us in our party, we each claimed a wing of the place to ourselves and went into the town of Vail to fill the cupboards with gourmet delights and the finest wines and liquor that would sustain us for our week in this winter paradise.

The times, being what they were and in the rash rationalization of 20-somethings world-wide, we also acquired quite a few *party-favors* or *recreational substances* to help while away the crisp, cold winter nights.

I have to admit that we had an absolute ball that week, skiing in Vail, Breckenridge and Telluride during the day and at night, getting high as kites and dancing the night away in the many nightclubs that catered to the mostly young, well-connected and wealthy clientele that frequented the surrounding area.

There is an old saying that claims, *God watches over drunks and fools*. That saying could be amended to include *drunks, fools and reckless youths*! Along with some high quality marijuana (pun absolutely intended!), we had acquired some purportedly quite potent *magic mushrooms*, which we proceeded to indulge in while the moon waxed full over the mountains surrounding our cosy vacation home. The magnificent views, the amazingly clean colours given off by the blazing fire, copious amounts of marijuana, cognac and 'shrooms and a late night hit of a tab of acid, lulled us into a deep and thoroughly relaxing sleep.

The next morning, we headed out for yet another day on the slopes. While both Jane and Konrad were expert skiers, I on the other hand was decidedly not! I had graduated from the beginners or *bunny runs* and I could, on my best days, remain upright on the decidedly less difficult intermediary runs. However, my mind was obviously still clouded by all of the substances I had imbibed the night before and I was busy admiring the view passing below me as I ascended the mountain in a chair lift; Konrad and Jane having gone on a few chairs before me.

When I reached the summit, I, without thought or hesitation, dismounted from the lift and took off in full pursuit of my two friends, already making head-way down the mountain. Unbeknown to me, the slope on which Jane and Konrad had just vanished from sight was a Black Diamond run, a steep descent that is reserved for expert skiers only. In addition, this particular downhill run also featured moguls, basically mounds of snow the size of Volkswagens forming large bumps in the snow to add to the degree of difficulty in navigating the course. Ignorance is bliss, and as I stated earlier, God was truly watching over this fool that day as I sped downhill hell-bent for leather after my unsuspecting friends, who were quickly coming into my sight-line.

I hit the first mogul with quite a lot of speed and with a bone-shattering jar to my system. My knees were instantly compacted into my chin and sprung back down like the coiled springs of an out of control vehicle and gathered speed as I once again made contact with the ground. At this point, I experienced an out-of-body visualization of myself hurtling downhill as if a racer in the Winter Olympics, so strongly that I was in fact imitating all of the moves I had seen so many times on the TV. I was completely engulfed in the moment and the thought that I couldn't or shouldn't be attempting this, never entered my altered state of mind.

By the time I shot past an extremely shocked Konrad and Jane, who had paused downhill to laugh about something or other, I was going about 60 miles an hour shouting, "WHEEEEEEEE!!!!!" like a complete and utter idiot. I could faintly hear both of them gasp, "WTF? TAL?" as I zoomed past them, intent only upon staying up-right on my by now furiously vibrating skis. I noted that they had both taken off in hot pursuit of their crazed companion and spotting the bottom of the hill approaching with lightning speed I put all of my energy and concentration into bringing this wild-ride to an end that did not involve any broken bones or a body-cast.

Moments before Konrad and Jane appeared by my side shouting out, "STOP! PLOW! PLOW! STOP!" I paralleled my skis to the ground, crouched into a semi-sitting position and with a dramatic flourish worthy of the moment and throwing up a sheet of powdered-snow, ground to a semi-dignified halt. It was only after I came to a complete stop that I slid un-ceremoniously to the ground all the while listening to my friends simultaneously shouting, "Are you out of your fucking mind? You could have been killed!" I raised my head off the snow, removed my goggles and said, "Dayum ... I didn't think that I would make it!" After looking back up the slope and at the height from which I had just descended, I added, "I will NEVER, EVER, DO THAT AGAIN".

Later in the afternoon, after many drinks had coursed through our veins we all decided that I owed my life (and all of my limbs) to the kindly intervention of a benevolent deity and that none of us would ever ski under the influence of anything stronger than a cup of coffee again in this lifetime.

CHAPTER 25

H.R.H KONA "QUEEN OF THE LHR BASE"

Among a flight service base populated with Nordic goddesses, one exotic and stunning beauty stood out from the crowd.

Kona Massqui was a poised, elegant and statuesque socialite, whose chic style invariably made her the centre of attention wherever she happened to be. The fact that Kona was a bona-fide African princess only added to her mystic and allure. Both Kona and her identical twin sister, Yuku, had been fashion models in NYC before joining Pan Am. Her innate regal bearing offset by exquisite cheek bones, wide-set eyes, a luscious mouth and enviable figure made an awe-inspiring impact on everyone she encountered. In a nod to her lineage, she was affectionately nicknamed the *Queen of the LHR base.*

I first met Kona at one of Konrad's stylish dinner parties and, like everyone else, was immediately mesmerised. At nearly six feet tall, wearing the most amazing jewels to accentuate her incredible designer attire and surrounded by sycophants, Kona was the object of everyone's attention. When we were finally introduced, I gave her a kiss on each cheek and quipped, "Your Royal Highness, what a pleasure it is to make your acquaintance." This elicited a deep and full-throttled burst of laughter from Kona, instantly kindling a friendship that would be decades long.

A few months after our introduction, Kona invited me to move into her luxuriously furnished three-bedroom flat on a fashionable street near Kensington Palace and I happily accepted. With Kona's impeccable connections this was my entrée into London's social elite. Kona entertained on a level that I imagined had only existed in the life style pages of high-end magazines. I can honestly say that I have never consumed such vast amounts of champagne and caviar during the three fantastic years I was privileged to share her fabulous lifestyle and luxurious abode.

Although extremely well-connected, Kona was not without *street-smarts* and did not suffer arrogance, ill-manners or fools lightly. The fact that she was stunningly beautiful, well-educated and fluent in three languages made her the darling of the social scene and when she wasn't flying off to some exciting destination for Pan Am, she could be found in one of London's famed nightspots.

I had just returned from an Oslo, Norway, layover and was sleeping soundly, when I was awakened by the sound of shattering glass. Earlier that evening, Kona and a Swedish friend of hers, Briggitta, had gone out on a double date with two diplomats from an oil-rich nation and apparently the evening had not gone as the two men had planned. Rushing from my bedroom into our lounge, I was startled by the sight of Kona, looking like an outraged Valkyrie, towering over a cowering middle aged Lothario, holding the remains of a cloisonné vase in one hand, while furiously shouting "GET the FUCK OUT!" I entered the room in time to witness a smartly dressed middle-eastern gentleman rubbing his now bruised and rapidly swollen head as he grabbed his companion and beat a hasty retreat out the front door.

As soon as he exited our flat and ran sheepishly into a cold and drizzly London night, both Kona and Briggitta doubled over in fits of laughter. When she regained her breath and could speak Kona, taking in my bug-eyed expression, explained, "that uncouth bastard though that he could have his way with me for the price of a dinner! On top of that, the prick ripped the strap of my Givenchy gown! I wanted to smash his idiotic skull in!" Quickly regaining her composure Kona opened up a bottle of champagne and raucously toasted the fact that "the price of pussy just went up!", while we all howled with laughter at the manner in which she had quenched her amorous suitor's advances and how he had, literally, fled into the night.

I always looked forward to and enjoyed the flights that we worked together if for no other reason than to observe the effect that Kona had on unruly or boisterous passengers. We were working a trip together with Konrad, returning to London from Amsterdam with a plane load of rowdy English football fans. The drunken party animals were well on the way to becoming a public nuisance when Konrad and I watched in amazement as Kona emerged from the First Class cabin and slowly and deliberately walked down first one side of the plane, then the other, narrowing her eyes in displeasure and disgust and glaring at each inebriated man in her sight, leaving a trail of silent, open-mouthed imbeciles in her wake.

Astonished, both Konrad and I asked her how she rendered the group of louts speechless. Raising her eyebrows and in her lilting most gracious tone she replied, "I gave them my 'I'm going to chill the SHIT in you look'. It works every time." My mother is the only other person I know that can accomplish this feat and even though I have attempted to replicate her sound deadening immobilizing glare over the years, I have yet to succeed in quieting an unruly mob with a single glance.

I have known several sets of twins over the years and while in outward appearances they may appear mirror images of one another there is usually a quirk or personality trait that marks their individuality. Kona and Yoko were so much alike that an outside observer would be hard-pressed to distinguish one from the other. However, having lived with Kona on a daily basis, I knew her personality traits and (usually) could work out just which twin I was dealing with. Kona was definitely the more dominant of the two; her assertive personality always present and in the forefront of her interactions with people. Yoku was far more subdued and possessed a much more relaxed and laid-back personality. Yoku was based at JFK in New York City and although they were in the same training class, Kona had drawn a higher seniority by number from her twin, perhaps reflecting the fact that she was the older of the two by a few minutes.

I had just walked through the door of the flat after a particularly gruelling flight back from New Delhi, when a surprisingly chipper and beaming Kona greeted me with a warm smile and a kiss.

This in itself was not out of the ordinary, but I was shocked when she handed me a Mimosa and offered to make me a huge breakfast of eggs, toast, potatoes, tomatoes and bacon and I began to wonder if something was amiss. Moving closer, I raised my eyebrows quizzically and sputtered, "Yuko, is that you?" She almost fell over laughing and asked, "How did you know?" I replied that in the first place, while Kona would have downed a glass of champagne from me, she would NEVER make a drink for me before seeing to her own beverage. She also would NEVER have ruined a manicure by cooking breakfast, for anyone, before noon at the earliest!

Over the delicious breakfast that she had prepared for us, Yoku told me that Kona had taken a flight to New York and was spending the next week shopping at all of her favourite haunts. Since Yoku had that period of time off from duty, she had switched places with her sister and worked the flight back to London under Kona's name! I was dumbfounded, amazed and jealous at the audacity of their ruse. Because of the close proximity I had with Kona, I was the only person capable of noticing any difference between the two and no one was ever aware of their switch apart from the three of us. After a week spent on retail therapy in New York, Kona worked back to London with Yoku returning (as herself) on the outbound trip to JFK. From that day on, whenever I happened to cross paths with Yoku, I would wink and in a stage whisper say, "Hey Kona, guuuurrrrrllll, what's new?" bringing a guffaw from both of us.

My adventures with both of these lovely Massqui sisters were fantastic, fun and far too numerous to list in these pages. I owe them both my everlasting gratitude for introducing me to high society and the fine pleasures in life: Petrossiani (caviar), Prada and any designer based in Paris you can think of. *MERCI BEAUCOUP MES SOEURS!*

CHAPTER 26

CELEBRITY SIGHTINGS

Pan Am was the premier American air carrier in the '70s and '80s and as such, we frequently carried a multitude of VIPs in our First Class cabin. Since private jets were not the norm in those days, it was not unusual to encounter political heavy-weights, musicians at the zenith of their careers, clothing designers and the models who made their clothes famous, authors and journalists heralding the Zeitgeist, celebrated chefs and of course a panoply of exalted actors and actresses.

Since many of the actors and actresses we came into contact with were legendary movie stars from the Golden Age of Hollywood, they invariably had about them an aura of glamour not always associated with contemporary film stars. While based in London-Heathrow, it was my pleasure to have met and served true screen legends in our First Class cabin on flights between LHR and our ports of call in the US. Possibly the most thrilling encounter was on a flight from JFK to LHR with her Serene Highness Princess Grace of Monaco and her husband Prince Rainer. Not only was Princess Grace more beautiful in person, but both she and her husband were charming and charismatic, treating everyone in the crew with respect and kindness, a trait that seems a lost virtue with the mileage-plus passengers of today.

Everyone has heard reports of rude and obnoxious passengers, but in my experiences with the public it seemed that the most famous people I encountered were the most secure and therefore the most polite and personable.

I will never forget serving the legendary John Wayne and his gorgeous wife Pilar on a flight from LHR to LAX. The *Duke* could not have been more gracious in his interactions with the crew and passengers who happened to be travelling with him in First Class. He truly was a star in every sense of the word.

Other luminaries that left a lasting and pleasant impression were Burt Lancaster and Kirk Douglas and their wives travelling from LAX to the Cannes Film Festival, laughing and joking their way across the Atlantic and delighting everyone they met. In the tail end of her 6th marriage to Senator John Warner of Virginia, Elizabeth Taylor travelled with us on a flight from LHR to Washington, DC, Dulles.

Liz dazzled us all with her rancorous wit and humour and I can still hear her loud, braying laugh as she regaled us with tales of *old Hollywood*. That and the fact that she was wearing an 8.24 carat (ruby surrounded by 8 large diamonds) ring, a gift from Richard Burton, completely overwhelmed me. I was so bedazzled by her rock that she quipped, "Here Honey, why don't you wear it to pour coffee and tea?" I assured her that it suited her perfectly manicured hands much more than it ever would a mere mortal with sausage fingers. Miss Taylor assured us that she had made a valiant attempt to fit-in with Washington society as a senator's wife, but had found the hypocrisy and posturing of the Washington power brokers and their wives stifling and that she couldn't wait to *get 'back home' to Hollywood and civilization.*

The upper decks of Pan Am's fleet of 747s were unique in that they featured a dining room that was converted into a First Class lounge after the dinner service was completed. I was engrossed in preparing the meals for the eight passengers I would be serving, when I was startled by the familiar face and booming voice of world renowned chef Julia Child. Emerging suddenly at the top of the spiral staircase, she almost made me drop the roast I was seasoning when she bellowed, "Cheerio, I do hope that you don't mind my meddling." As if I could possibly broach any objection to a cultural icon giving me advice! Recovering somewhat I introduced myself and explained that I was the galley attendant that evening. "Wonderful" she replied, "let's see what we have to work with shall we?"

The galley (kitchen) was located just aft of the spiral staircase from the main deck and was quite a compact area. Miss Child was well over six foot and while not overweight was quite a robust woman. The two of us crammed into that tiny space must have been quite a sight. I was not only in absolute awe of her culinary skills as a chef but was a huge fan of her television program *Dinner with Julia* and was flabbergasted that I was face to face with one of my all-time idols. The fact that I was being given a one on one lesson from one of the most popular chefs in the world, in the confines of an airline galley no less, was something I will never forget.

In those days everything was made from scratch. Meats, fowl and fish as well as vegetables had to be prepared to order; quite a feat at 39,000 ft. Surveying the limited condiments that were in the galley, Miss Child concocted a paste of Dijon mustard, red wine, salt, pepper and of course butter and liberally covered the roast I was about to cook. "Since I will be having the fillet of Dover sole I think we will sauté this fish with a liberal cup of white wine, some butter, salt and pepper. That should do quite nicely don't you think?" After all of the vegetables had been given a touch of butter and placed in the ovens, Miss Child declared the meal preparation complete and descended to the main deck while the FAs prepared the tables with flowers, china and silverware befitting a "first class restaurant". Needless to say my meals that night were a resounding success with numerous comments of how perfectly seasoned and delicious the cuisine by Pan Am had become.

After dinner was served and the area had once again be converted to the First Class lounge, Miss Child returned to relax over a glass of sherry and introduced me to her husband Paul. I took the opportunity to thank her profusely for her "master class" and was thrilled when she invited me to join her and her husband. I spent an hour or so in her company as she reminisced about her amazing life making that moment one of the highlights of my career. My face never ceases to light-up when I hear that unmistakable voice saying "BON APPETIT"!

In the fall of 1979 I was working the First Class cabin on a flight from LAX to LHR when an animated buzz of excited chatter filled the air.

Mark Hamill, one of the main stars of the hugely popular film *Star Wars*, was traveling in First Class headed to Norway to film *Episode V - The Empire Strikes Back.* Like the rest of the crew, I was a huge fan of George Lucas' film and was thrilled to have *Luke Skywalker* as my *guest* for the 11 hr 25 min trip to London.

After the meal service was completed and most of the passengers in First Class had retired for the night, we struck up a conversation and discovered that we had much in common. Besides being the same age, we both shared a passion for fast cars and he was delighted when I shared photos of my 1976 TR6 that was my pride and joy at the time. In the winter of 1977, Mark had been in a serious accident while driving his BMW in Los Angeles that left him with a fractured nose and a left cheekbone requiring several hours of facial reconstructive surgery. Filming of the sequel had been postponed until his injuries had healed and he was now on his way to Norway to resume work on the second film in the series. Like everyone involved in the film, Mark could not divulge any of the plot or storyline, but assured me that he was more than ready to take up his light saber and rejoin the rebels battling the evil Galactic Empire.

Mark Hamill was a complete delight to be around with absolutely none of the affectations or artifice that he could have easily adopted as the star of a mega-hit film and we ended up chatting through most of the flight. Upon landing in London, he gave me a bear hug, wishing me safe travels. It was like saying farewell to an old friend.

When the movie opened in 1980, I was one of the first of my acquaintances to see the finished project and like countless fans around the world, was thrilled with the results. It took very little speculation on my part to realize just how the film's writers had incorporated Mark's accident into the storyline. The snowy terrain of Norway evolved into the ice planet *Hoth* where the rebels were in hiding from the forces of evil, led by Darth Vader. In the film,

Luke Skywalker is attacked by a *wampa*, a creature that closely resembled a yeti or *Abominable Snowman*. Of course, anyone familiar with the plot knows that Luke uses *the force* to get out of this predicament and ultimately triumphs over the creature.

Given the circumstances causing the delay in the filming, I'd like to think the *wampa* attack was included in the film to explain the slight differences in Marks's appearance that were the after-effects of his car crash. Whatever the case may be, I will never forget and always treasure my up close and personal encounter with a truly gifted actor and outstanding role model for legions of fans, just like myself!

CHAPTER 27
NO GOOD DEED!

On Pan Am's around the world flight one, I had been *juniored* into working the FC galley position. As the F/A with the least seniority on the crew, I was unlucky enough to be working with Gertrude Weiss, a notoriously strict and authoritarian Teutonic purser who was the personification of a harridan! With her thin, pinched face, severely plucked eyebrows and permanently down-turned mouth, she was a doppelgänger for Margaret Hamilton, the actress who portrayed *The Wicked Witch of the West* in the film classic *The Wizard of Oz.*

I'm certain that at some point in her distant youth, Miss Weiss, as she insisted upon being addressed (behind her back the crew referred to her as "Frau Bluecher" the villainous character from Mel Brook's film *Young Frankenstein*), was a relatively attractive woman, however years of a bitter disposition had taken its toll resulting in a face that did little to invite warmth and quite a lot to instil fear! Gertrude was infamous throughout the LHR base for her collection of flamboyant wigs which sat precariously upon her head, enhancing a still enviously slender body for which she was justifiably proud.

Gertrude had just finished barking out orders for the manner in which she expected her presentation cart (silverware, stemware, cutlery, linens etc.) to be prepared, when she turned her back to me, marching imperiously down the aisle to seat 1K, where a call button had summoned her. In those days the call button was situated directly over the seat and was a pull-down mushroom-shaped device that when activated, illuminated a light directly over the seat while simultaneously activating a call chime in the galley alerting the crew that assistance was required at that particular seat.

Since the galley was located in the rear of the First Class cabin, I glanced over my shoulder just in time to observe Gertrude bending stiffly down from her waist inquiring what was needed from the passenger seated in 1K. Nodding curtly and assuring the gentleman that she would be right back, Gertrude snapped back into an upright position and proceeded to goose-step her way back to the galley. Unfortunately as she turned her body to head back to the galley where I was watching, her flame-colored wig was snagged by the call button, which she had NOT pushed in (thereby silencing the chime) and like a marionette whose string was caught, her wig was left dangling above the seat. She had taken several steps before she realized her predicament.... and stood frozen with shock in the middle of the aisle. Before she could make a hasty retrieval and retreat however, I burst out into an uncontrollable fit of raucous, loud GUFFAWS... doubling over with tears running down my face, unable to contain my undisguised glee! She looked rather like a recently-plucked chicken, her wisps of unruly greying hair standing up like an electric shock wave as she stormed past me, wig in hand... slamming the lavatory door behind her.

Unfortunately for me, not only had I drawn attention to her plight, but laughter being contagious, it had caused titters of barely suppressed giggles to sweep through the First Class cabin.

When she emerged from the lavatory five minutes later, her wig, now adjusted to a semblance of its former state, sat atop a beet-red, thunderous face. Her lips pursed into even more of a slit, her eyes narrowed and blazing with vitriol, she hissed: "ARE ....YOU ...QUITE ...FINISHED???!!" As I was stifling another outburst of laughter at that moment I could only attempt to force a straight-faced expression....and rapidly nodded in the affirmative. Gertrude huffed and puffed like the dragon she was and with a theatrical "HMPH!" strode like a Valkyrie out of the galley, but not before fixing me with a molten glare that by rights should have struck me dead on the spot!

The second her back was turned, I collapsed into an uncontrollable fit of giggles.

I was soon to learn a valuable lesson; NEVER, EVER underestimate the wrath of a humiliated, vindictive and spiteful older woman!

We were on the segment of the trip that serviced Frankfurt to Istanbul and the customer service representative had been delayed while escorting an elderly, wheelchair-bound German woman from the aircraft to the customs hall. As we were soon scheduled to depart for the trip to Istanbul, I offered to take the woman at least as far as the immigrations hall in the hope of encountering one of our ground agents along the way. With a curt nod of her head Gertrude acknowledged my request and I set off at a brisk pace, pushing the wheelchair of the fragile *fraulein* as quickly as I dared, and headed for the customs hall.

About halfway to my destination, I came across a Pan Am ground agent and after receiving a heartfelt *Danke schoen* and a peck on the cheek from the old dear, I headed back to the gate where we were shortly scheduled to depart. With a quick glance down at my watch to assure that I would make it back before boarding had commenced, I picked up my pace, trotting back through the departure lounge. I have to point out that Pan Am's gates were located in a vast circle with separate gates adjacent to the next, like spokes on a giant wheel. As each of the extended jet bridges was identical, I did not pay much attention as I strolled, now nonchalantly whistling, down the passageway and onto the plane.

Since each airplane was laid out in the same format, I did not realize that anything was amiss until I went to the first class closet in the nose of the plane to hang up my jacket. Just as I was about to walk back up the aisle to resume my galley position, a brunette F/A, whom I had not seen on the previous leg, looked up from where SHE was preparing the galley and observing my ID badge smiled and chirped, "Oh...! Are you joining us to work this flight or are you dead-heading..?" Puzzled I replied, "Ummm that's funny, I was just about to ask YOU the same thing!" Now thoroughly confused, I let out a long breath and said, "Hang on, this IS the flight to Istanbul, isn't it?" A sudden sinking sensation that had begun to broil in my stomach turned into outright dread when she replied, "NO honey, THIS is flight 2 to JFK!" I broke into a cold sweat and my face turned ashen. Simultaneously we both shouted: "OH SHIT!" when the realization hit me that the flight I was SUPPOSED to be on was departing from the gate just next door and to the LEFT of the aircraft I was now bolting from.

With sweat pouring down my face I rounded the corner racing full-speed ahead just in time to see the aircraft door shut on flight 1 and the agent beginning to pull the jet way away from the now departing airplane. Screaming over the roar of the engines I frantically explained that I was meant to be WORKING on that flight, at which point she halted the pull-back and called the cockpit of flight 1 to alert them of the situation.

Tense moments later, the plane SLOWLY returned to the docking bay and the aircraft door was opened by non other than Gertrude, her razor-thin lips distorting her face with a barely disguised semblance of a smile. I was breathlessly sputtering, "YOU KNEW where I was ... WHY did you let them close the door???!!!" She bared her teeth and with a reptilian hiss replied, "But my DEAR.... I thought you were on board in the lavatory. At any rate the CAPTAIN would like a word with you... NOW ...in the cockpit!"

As angry as I was with that evil bitch, I was nevertheless literally trembling when I climbed the spiral staircase leading upstairs to the cockpit of the 747, with each step feeling like I was headed to the guillotine for my summary execution. The cockpit door was open and Captain Frantz was leaning back in his seat, craning his neck to glare at me as I gulped... almost tripping over my feet, and stumbled into the cockpit and certain doom. "WELL ..." he intoned in a baritone only heard in movies, "What have you got to say for yourself?" In a torrent of words I explained that I was in fact attempting to do a good dead and in my haste to get back had inadvertently boarded the aircraft next door and ..."ENOUGH!!!" he said. "I gather that this was presumably an innocent mistake" After a lecture on the cost of fuel he might have burned had he succeeded in taxing away from the gate, he let me off the hook with a stern rebuke. Light-headed with relief, I returned to my work position at door 1R and after glaring at Gertrude with a look I hoped would cause her heart to fail, fastened my seat belt and prepared to take off for Istanbul.

Word of the incident of course spread like wild-fire amongst the crew and everyone was in complete agreement that I had almost been *done in* by the spiteful machinations of our EVIL HAG of a chief purser. As I sat stewing with anger, I had to admit that the situation could have been worse had I missed the flight altogether and could quite possibly have been terminated for dereliction of my duties. At that point I swallowed my pride, vowing to myself never ever to laugh or poke fun at the misfortunes of my flying partner ever again. Well, not publicly that is!

In a twist of fate five years later, I transferred to the LAX base and ended up becoming best friends and house-mates with Lisa Frantz, a drop-dead gorgeous blonde, who just happened to be the daughter of the captain who had put the fear of God in me. Whenever I saw him, either working a flight or when he visited our home in Los Angeles, we always shared a hearty laugh about the day he almost caused me to shit my pants!

CHAPTER 28

FLYING IN STYLE

My most hectic celebrity moment occurred on a flight from LAX to LHR in 1981. I was thrilled to welcome aboard one of the most famous actresses of the 20th century, Gloria Swanson, whose career had spanned cinema from its inception with silent films through to the Golden Age of Hollywood. The apogee of Miss Swanson's incredibly lengthy career was her portrayal of Norma Desmond, a silent film star confronting the demise of her career in Billy Wilder's *Sunset Boulevard*, a film cult favourite. At the time that I met her, Ms Swanson was 82 years old but appeared to only be in her early 60s – if that. Ms Swanson was a complete delight and an extremely charming woman, who was thrilled that I had committed her most memorable lines from *Sunset Boulevard* to memory and roared with laughter when I informed her (mimicking her of course) that I was "ready for my close-up ... Mr DeMille".

I was chief purser and shortly before landing at Heathrow, I was in the upper-deck lounge and was completing the customs forms required by Her Majesty's government regarding inbound liquor on board the aircraft. This tedious task was abruptly interrupted by Helene, a young and very junior F/A from Detroit, who stumbled up the stairs and into the cabin distraught and dishevelled blurting out, "Tal, come quick! ... Ms Swanson is DEAD!" Throwing the paper work aside I dashed down the spiral staircase and bolted to seat 1A, where an apparently comatose Gloria Swanson, head thrown back, mouth agape and eyes wide open, was seated. Calming myself and with a trembling Helene leaning over my shoulder, I called out, "Ms Swanson, Ms Swanson?" while reaching in to touch her carotid artery to see if I could determine the presence of a pulse. Just as my hand was about to make contact with her neck Ms Swanson flinched and let out a loud drawn-out snore. Both stifling a scream, Helene and I jumped about three feet in the air, startled completely out of our wits. When we recovered from out shock, I noticed that the intake of breath and the rising of her chest strongly indicated signs of life. It occurred to me that Ms Swanson had merely been in a deep sleep, hence her open mouth and because of numerous *improvements to her appearance*, could not fully close her eyes.

Thanking God that disaster had been averted and that a film legend was still among the living, I placed my hand over my still racing heart and slowly tip-toed back to the confines of the upper deck lounge.

CHAPTER 29

ALMOST THE END OF DÉTENTE

One of the most exciting destinations for Pan Am F/As in the '80s was Moscow, the capital city of Russia's Soviet Empire. In those days we enjoyed a lengthy layover in the centre of the city, in the Art Nouveau palatial Metropolis Hotel.

It was the middle of February and the evening temperature was around -10C (14F). My crew and I had enjoyed an incredible evening at the Bolshoi ballet followed by some serious consumption of Blini's, thin Russian pancakes filled with sour cream, and countless tonnes of caviar, downed with obscene amount of chilled vodka.

We continued drinking vodka far into the wee hours of the morning and as we were literally toasted and no one could either walk, let alone make it back to their respective rooms, we decided to have a sleepover in the corner room in which we were all congregated.

Even though we were (for the most part anyway) fully clothed and the heat was cranked up as far as it could go, in our inebriated state we took down the heavy draperies that were covering the windows, in order to add to the bed coverings that we had spread out on the floor. Somehow or other the topic of spying and eaves-dropping by the KGB on American subjects came about and one of our drunken revellers felt what appeared to be a large microphone or *listening device* hidden under the ornate, oriental carpet that covered the floor we were gathered on.

"Aha ... I knew it!" was the response of Gilberto, one of our intrepid group, who proceeded to attempt to pry the *listening device* from the floor with a knife left over from room service. After several minutes futilely spent worrying at the bolt holding the metal plate to the floor, we gave up and fell into an exhausted drunken stupor.

We had all happened to fall asleep in the second floor room that unbeknown to out imbecilic crew was directly over a ballroom/conference room in the corner of the first floor. The *listening device* that we had not succeeded (thankfully) in prying loose was the bolted base of a crystal chandelier hanging in the centre of the room directly below us. It was not until hours later when dead sober we were awakened by the cleaning-staff who noticed the missing curtains from the window and asked if we had "heard or noticed anything unusual during the night?" Bald-facedly lying, we all assumed the most innocent expressions that we could muster, and making certain that the carpet had indeed covered out misdeeds of the previous night, replied "Nyet!"

Later that afternoon as we were checking out of the hotel for our trip back to London, we sheepishly peeked into the ballroom where we all took notice of a repair crew retightening a bolt that had somehow mysteriously been loosened during the night.

When we were once again safely air-borne, we all collectively breathed a sigh of relief that a decade of a hard-won and delicate detente had not been *shattered* by the actions of a drunken crew.

CHAPTER 30

THE END OF AN ERA

The year 1985 began with disconcerting rumours regarding the financial security and viability of Pan Am. It was unthinkable to me that the future of America's most prestigious and storied air carrier would be in jeopardy, let alone in danger of vanishing altogether.

Nevertheless, hedging all my bets and preparing myself for the worst-case scenario, I decided it was best to head back to the US mainland and transfer to Pan Am's Los Angeles base. Even though I had grown to truly love England I figured if I had to indeed start anew the perpetually warm and sunny climate of California would not be a bad place to start.

The fact that dear friends such as Ann-Marie Berryman and Brenda Bagsely had recently moved to Los Angeles was further motivation to leave the perpetually grey buildings, grey climate, grey food and grey people of my beloved London for sunny California.

Konrad had also decided to flee what could be considered as a sinking ship and headed to an even more tropical climate transferring from London to Pan Am's base in Honolulu, Hawaii. This sealed the deal for me, as my best friend would only be a five-hour flight away from the mainland, located in a tropical paradise and the party potential was endless.

My first six months or so living in Los Angeles was framed by a deep sense of culture shock. Whereas Englishmen, Londoners in particular, entertained on a grand level, mostly in private residences and invariably dressed to impress at all times, Angelinos were laid-back to the point of somnolence, lacking any sense of dress-style other than shorts, t-shirts and flip-flops. I was appalled!

Shedding my inhibitions along with several layers of clothing, I slowly learned to adapt to the beach culture that prevailed in LA - unless a *red carpet* was involved, when glamour once again reared its stylish head. Shortly after my arrival, the other shoe did indeed drop, and Pan Am announced the plan to sell off its Pacific route to United Airline, the largest domestic US carrier at the time.

Mergers and acquisitions are never subtle easy transitions. The melding of Pan Am's aloof and haughty F/As, with the more casual and less sophisticated *stews* of United Airlines, was a turbulent affair that dragged out for three years. When the issue of seniority was finally addressed, I had lost a total of five years by being slotted into UAL's F/A list. As a result, hurt feelings, mistrust and *bad blood* circulated among both groups for quite a while.

For the first three years of the transition, the 1202 Pan Am F/As who were part and parcel of the Pacific routes acquired by UAL, were relegated, for the most part, to flying mostly domestic (US) routes with the occasional Hawaiian island trip thrown in for good measure.

I have to state that this is old news and past history, water well and truly under the bridge. And I have now spent more years flying with UAL than Pan American and have acquired numerous life-long friends in the process.

However, the first three years were in fact quite turbulent.

UAL had specialised in flying passengers between mainland US and the Hawaiian islands, which they manifested as *our little corner of the world*. F/As were required to wear brightly coloured floral attire on the Hawaiian flights, the ladies in floor length *muumuus*, baby blue polyester material decorated with pink and canary yellow flowers. I like to say lots of *naghus gave up their hides* in order for us to look so stylish. The males were dressed in long-sleeved jackets sporting the identical floral motif of their female counter-parts. The Pan-Am girls liked to retort that we gave up our white linen gloves for blue rubber ones.

I was working a Honolulu trip with Ann-Marie and we car-pooled together to the airport for our early morning departure. We had stopped to fill-up Ann-Marie's car with gas in order to avoid doing so on our late night return.

Anne-Marie had gone inside the station to purchase a coffee, attired in her brightly-hued floor-length polyester muumuu and I was standing beside the car, in what I referred to as my *Ferdinand Marcos* house-boy coat, when an elderly gentleman pumping gas next to me glanced up at our matching outfits and quizzically enquired, "Are you two in a singing group?" Without missing a beat, I looked up and quipped, "Yep, that's right, we're the new Christy Minstrels" - a folk-singing group popular in the 1960s. Choking on her coffee, Ann-Marie gave the man a dazzling smile, said, "Pleased to meet you" and dashed into the car.

We laughed our asses off all the way to the airport.

CHAPTER 31

COLLOQUIL DISASTERS

Time, as they say, heals all wounds and three years after our merger, the dust had settled and a semblance of normalcy returned to our flying careers. I was now able to return to more of our international destinations in the Pacific; Tokyo, Hong Kong, Tahiti, South Korea, New Zealand and my personal favourite, Australia.

I had fallen in love with Australia when I had first spotted the sails of the world famous Opera House and the iconic Harbour Bridge on a holiday in Sydney, sometime in the early '80s. The spectacular harbour with its stunning architecture, the Opera House located in Circular Quay chief among them, coupled with the most hospitable people on the planet, completely and thoroughly won me over. In addition to incredibly beautiful beaches populated with stunning specimens, Sydney featured some the best cuisine and restaurants in the world.

Venturing into the local pubs, however, I soon discovered that ignorance of the local colloquialisms could result in quite awkward, if not down-right embarrassing situations. Our layover hotel was located at the entrance to Kings Cross, at that time an area notorious for its bawdy and risqué night clubs and jazz haunts. It was populated by enterprising prostitutes of all persuasions, rowdy sailors on shore leave and a spattering of wide-eyed tourists looking to be shocked and entertained. I had just left a smoke-filled, stuffy and stiflingly hot underground jazz venue and was headed back to the hotel, when the throbbing strains of disco lured me into a club filled to the rafters with scantily clad women and shirtless men gyrating to Patti Labelle's *Lady Marmalade*. This seemed like a perfect spot to dance the night away and I soon joined the crowd on the dance floor. Forty minutes later and sweating profusely, I headed for the bar. Just as I was about to order a beer from the barman a blonde-haired six foot tall bare-chested, heavily muscled *Aussie* leaned over and getting close to my ear in order to be heard over the blaring music shouted, "CAN I get you some PISS mate?"

I was sure that I hadn't heard him correctly so, frowning, I turned to him and yelled, "What?"

"Do you want more piss?" he replied and when I was certain that I hadn't misconstrued him, I gave him a filthy disgusted look and shoved my way out of the bar and back into the crowded streets. It wasn't until the next morning when I was recounting my near-miss in what I assumed was a den of inequity, that my friends laughingly informed me that *piss* was Australian for an alcoholic beverage and the guy was politely offering me a drink.

In quick succession I learned not to take other Aussie utterances at face value. Certain otherwise quite ordinary and innocent American phrases took on quite a different connotation when applied down under. Even if you were so full that another morsel of food would have caused your intestines to burst, you never declared that you were *stuffed*, as in Oz this connoted that you had just been screwed - literally!

Getting back to beverages, to say that you were *pissed* meant that you were well and truly drunk and on your ass and not angry with or about something, as in *pissed-off*. I learned to make a verbal distinction between the phrases *route* and *root* as in, "I'm flying the Sydney route this month", especially in conversations with the locals, as the former indicted a destination and the latter a *fuck*. Henceforth, I was never *rooted* to the spot in fascination with anything, without explaining in great detail exactly what I was referring to.

On a flight from LA to SYD, I was rounding the corner from the first class galley while carrying a full pot of hot coffee and heading into the aisle when I nearly collided with a lady who had just exited the restroom. In what I assumed was a polite way of saying, "Sorry but I almost burned your ass", I said, "Oops, sorry, I almost burned your fanny", eliciting a look of horror and shock on her face as she quickly backed away amid raucous burst of laughter from two gentlemen who happened to be standing nearby. When they could wipe the tears of laughter from their eyes they explained to me that, "Mate, you just told that lady you almost burned her PUSSY!" They kindly took the time to explain to me that a *fanny* was Aussie slang for vagina. Mortified and embarrassed I quickly added that phrase to the ever-growing list of words to be avoided at all costs!

By far and away, the most glaring difference in Australian versus American grammar was the ever-present use of the *C* word by Australians in everyday casual conversations. I have been brought up surrounded by strong female figures, chief among them my mother and four sisters. Out of respect, courtesy, common sense and a strong sense of self-preservation, I would never under any circumstances use the *C* word in conversation. Not only for myself, but for my peers as well, this word was considered too un-couth and too vulgar to ever use in conversation. Period.

You can only imagine my utter and complete shock when at a fashionable dinner party in Bondi attended by mostly female Qantas FAs, one gorgeous buxom brunette turned to a girl seated directly across from her and shouted, "You fucking cunt, you got the trip I wanted!" My mouth gaped open in shock and my eyes bulged out of my head in horror when, to my utter confusion, the rest of my dinner companions roared with laughter! At home in America, not only would that phrase have been cause for swift retribution and a definite faux pas if not a *buzz kill*, in Australia it apparently represented a clever retort or at least humor when said amongst friends. I was doubly shocked and confused that a group of women, no matter how drunk or *loose* they were, would ever consent to the use of that word in their presence!

Slowly recovering my wits and wiping the spilled food from my shirt, I learned that the *C* word was not considered vulgar per se, but was banded about amongst friends in a light-hearted manner. I later discovered that the *C* word was even used as a description of endearment or high-praise as in so and so is a *mad cunt*, meaning a brilliant or great person. There is a saying that proclaims not everything translated travels well.

For me, the use of the *C* word has and always will constitute a slur and a breach in decorum too far for me to ever bridge. I think that when I'm really pissed-off, the *B* word or *bitch* will suffice to denote my displeasure.

CHAPTER 32

LITTLE CHOCOLATE MAN

Australia is a country of mermen and mermaids. Honestly, the entire population seemingly learns to swim before they can walk and toddlers can be found frolicking in the surf on any beach on any given day. Whether it's surfing, sailing, diving or paddle-boarding, if an activity is located near or on the ocean, you can guarantee that Aussies will be the most dominate feature on the horizon.

The gorgeous beaches that grace the shoreline of Sydney and its suburbs are a water enthusiast's paradise and are constantly busy with sun-worshippers, swimmers and surfers.

I grew up in Wisconsin and for the two months of the year that our frigid weather made it possible, I had learned to swim in the relatively placid waters of Lake Michigan. Now, although not the strongest ocean swimmer, I was determined to improve on my stamina and technique and went swimming whenever I got the chance. One particularly sunny and beautiful Sunday afternoon (or *arvo* in Oz speak), I found myself at Bondi Beach, one of Sydney's most spectacular beaches and a major tourist spot. The locals made a habit of swimming from the north rocks on the far left hand side of the beach, paralleling the shoreline to the rock-pool located directly opposite and half a mile away. An incredible restaurant and view point, Icebergs, was where swimmers later rewarded their efforts with a schooner of beer and some of the seafood the restaurant was famous for.

Northern end of Bondi Beach.

Unfortunately for me and countless other clueless tourists, the local population had grown up with a knowledge of the various signs and flags that dotted the shoreline denoting various ocean/surf conditions or signs of danger. Thus it was with complete ignorance of the diamond shaped yellow and black signs positioned along the beach, that I blithely dove into the somewhat choppy waters at Bondi's north rocks that day to begin my swim to Icebergs at the southern end of the beach for a well-deserved cold beverage.

My head was under-water, turning only to catch a deep breath and I imagined that my form was flawless as I kicked and took long strokes for the opposite shore. About a quarter of the way into my swim, humming to myself to break the monotony, I had just turned my head sideways from the water and was about to take a breath, when I noticed that the water surrounding me was churning furiously. Startled out of my wits, I raised my head from the water just as the voice of GOD in a strong Aussie accent loudly boomed overhead, "OUT OF THE WATER! OI! OUT OF THE WATER NOW! OI YOU ... LITTLE CHOCOLATE MAN ... I'M TALKING TO YOU!"

Simultaneously two things happened at once; my heart froze and the theme music from the film Jaws reverberated in my head. Glancing fervently around I saw a helicopter hovering mere feet above me, with an Aussie lifeguard, megaphone in hand, gesturing at me to head to shore, pronto.

To say that I was scared shitless would be the understatement of the century. All sense of form forgotten, I flailed and thrashed my way towards the beach, taking notice of the fact I was the only fool now in the water. I wanted to empty my bladder in the worst way but seemed to recall reading somewhere that the scent of urine as well as blood attracted sharks. I stroked and kicked for all I was worth with my feet beating a staccato behind me and my heart racing so fast I thought it would burst and fear had shrunken my testicles to the size of peanuts. If the Olympics had been on, I would have been a certainty to be on the medal podium and the tears streaming down my face would have been genuine and made for great television as I was quaking with fear!

I now had an audience exhorting me on to greater speed from the beach and breathing heavily, swallowing more seawater than could possibly be healthy, I swam as if my life depended on it for the safety of dry land. I could hear the blood pounding in my ear as I prayed the last thing I would feel on this earth would not be the excruciating pain of a Great White shark's jaws around any of my extremities.

By now the spectators were shouting, "Go Mate, Go!" as I thrashed my way to shore. Finally, when I was knee deep in the shallows, two lifeguards hauled my thoroughly exhausted, frightened chocolate ass out of the surf and dumped me unceremoniously onto the sand. Between heaving up gallons of seawater I could discern the lifeguards lecturing me, something to the effect of, "Mate, didn't you see the bloody signs, or hear the loud speaker? There was a bloody shark sighted out there!" When I had stopped shaking and could speak I whispered, "Sorry mate!" and collapsed in an exhausted heap on the sands of Bondi Beach.

I can't speak for other tourists but this *LA chocolate man* made it his business to memorize every warning sign and every flag ever posted at a beach in Australia from that day on.

CHAPTER 33

GETTING OUT OF DODGE

Either by happenstance of just plain bad luck, I have twice been an eyewitness to the fall of a government while I was on a layover in a country embroiled in turmoil.

The first incident occurred in Tehran, Iran, en-route to New Delhi, India, on Pan Am's round-the-world flight one. While there had been obvious signs of political unrest such as student protests and general strikes in the preceding months we had been flying into Tehran, there was nothing to indicate the rapid and abrupt change in the status-quo of the country in January of 1979. Our crew had landed in Tehran on January 14 and after resting, we dispersed throughout the city in our usual routine of scouring the local markets for the finely woven carpets the region was famous for, in addition to brass artifacts and tins of pistachios and my personal favorite, caviar. The evening ended in the ordinary manner with dinner and drinking followed by our feeble and hilarious attempts at belly dancing.

I awoke on the morning of January 15, slightly hung-over and had just drawn open the curtains to my window. I was admiring the beautiful vista of the snow covered Alborz Mountain ranges in the distance when I happened to glance down to the courtyard and was instantly shocked into hyper alertness by the sight of army tanks surrounding the perimeter of our layover location; the Inter-Continental Hotel. As if the sight of armored vehicles wasn't enough, moments later the loud and incessant ringing of the phone snapped me out of my stunned reverie. The captain, in a remarkably calm and authoritative manner, informed me that he had received orders from Pan Am dispatch in JFK that we would be evacuating our non-essential airport personnel, along with our regularly scheduled passengers later in the morning and to be prepared to depart for the airport within the hour.

My pulse racing, I dashed into the shower and spent the next 20 minutes or so frantically throwing everything I had in my possession into my suitcase, taking great care to stash all my jewelry and anything of value in the deepest recesses of my shaving kit.

Donning my uniform, I proceeded to rendezvous with the rest of my crew, all of whom were as startled as I was, in the lobby of the hotel, which was now thronged with disheveled and frantic patrons, some bordering on hysteria. In a scene reminiscent of the *Tower of Babel*, a mob of tourists crowded around the front desk all yelling in their respective languages, demanding to know just what the hell was going on. Our crew surreptitiously slipped through a service entrance and into a waiting van, which, after a tense negotiation with one of the tank officers, sped off towards Tehran Airport.

We drove straight onto the tarmac and hurriedly boarded the plane. Moments later, busloads of frightened passengers along with the aforementioned Pan Am airport staff members, their families and a few pets, filled the aircraft to capacity. In record-breaking time we secured all of our thoroughly stressed and exhausted passengers' belongings in the over-head bins and anxiously awaited word from the cockpit that the plane had been cleared for take-off.

Shortly thereafter, we sped down the runway and the wheels of the aircraft retracted into the belly of the plane. The entire aircraft erupted in whoops of joy and unmitigated relief! We gained altitude and headed for the peace, calm and safety of Frankfurt, Germany, away from the troubled city of Tehran in the soon-to-be Republic of Iran. The following day, in a coup orchestrated by a cadre of militant students and religious zealots, the Shah was deposed and fled Tehran to Paris and his new existence in exile.

My second and far more dramatic bout with the collapse of a government was in Beirut, Lebanon. The Phoenician Intercontinental Hotel was the location of our layovers in Beirut and was truly spectacular in every aspect. The luxurious and opulently appointed rooms and spacious balconies offered amazing vistas of the Mediterranean Sea and the bathrooms featured gold-plated fixtures in the shape of dolphins. The bar in the hotel was situated alongside and underneath the Olympic-sized swimming pool and offered a Plexiglas view of attractive swimmers moving lazily through the water.

Like Tehran, the situation in Lebanon was volatile. Skirmishes between Israel and Lebanon had been continually increasing following the invasion of Lebanon by Israel in June of 1982. Adding to the hornet's nest was an ongoing civil unrest between different religious factions, although the political unrest had quieted somewhat by the time I found myself once again working flight 1, headed to New Delhi on the round-the-world flight.

The night of April 17 began uneventfully. Myself and other members of the crew were enjoying a bottle of wine, admiring the sunset over the Mediterranean Sea on the balcony of my room in the Phoenician and engrossed in some mundane discussions about the day we had just spent water-skiing, when we observed arcs of bright lights in short bursts strewing through the sky not 100 meters from where we sat. It soon became clear to us that the steady, persistent bursts of light accompanied by a distinct retort were not a fireworks display but tracer bullets indicating a gun battle directly within our range of sight.

Horrified, we quickly extinguished the lights in the room and backed off the balcony and as far out of sight as we could. The ringing of the phone made us jump in alarm adding to the tension that was now palpable in the room. The station manager of Pan Am's Beirut operations was online and barked out orders for us to grab our passports and head to the hotel's maintenance elevators and meet in the kitchen as soon as possible. The rest of my crew immediately scattered to their respective rooms while I, still in total darkness except for the occasional firefight below me, crammed everything I could get my hands on into my luggage.

The second such incident in my career had made me an expeditious packer. The service elevator was soon filled with frantic crew members in various states of disarray and upon its hitting the ground floor, we rushed through the lobby and through the vast metal swinging doors of the kitchen. Once we had all gathered, our captain told us that a school bus had been commandeered and we were herded onto it headed immediately to the airport. The next 45 minutes were excruciatingly tense as we bounced and jerked our way down streets where gunfire could be heard, all the while lying on the floor of the bus, praying that we wouldn't be caught in the crossfire. After what seemed like an eternity and fraught with fear, we heard the captain ordering us off the bus and raced towards the silhouette of our darkened 747 parked on the tarmac. In the distance you could hear explosions as the night sky was briefly illuminated by bursts of fire. The plane was filled to capacity with all of our ground staff, ticket office staff and their relatives, pets and all of the belongings they could grab at a moment's notice. As soon as we had secured the cabin we took off in total darkness and away from the civil war raging below.

When we landed in Frankfurt on the morning of April 18, we learned to our horror that the US Embassy had been bombed by a suicide bomber, killing 63 people. It was the deadliest attack on a US diplomatic mission up to that time and marked the beginning of anti-US attacks by Islamic groups. From this day, I made a point of staying abreast of the political situation (especially of any signs of unrest) in any country that I might find myself visiting, either as a working crew member or as a tourist, and determined always to have an exit strategy in mind. I never got to see Beirut again and will always mourn the city that truly was one the most beautiful in the Middle East.

CHAPTER 34

"CHAMPAGNE!"

Several times in my life I've found that just being in the right place at the right time can lead to a serendipitous experience. I was on my way to holiday with a dear friend Paul Solomon and his family in Melbourne, Australia. This was the first week of November 1998 and I was excited to discover that Paul had arranged for me to attend the Melbourne Cup, a horse race akin to the Kentucky Derby, held on the first Tuesday in November and which quite literally brings the entire nation of Australia to a halt.

Shortly after take-off I had settled into my First Class seat and having decided to forgo the meal service in order to sleep the entire 14 hour flight to Australia, cupped a Zanax in my hand. At that moment, the extremely senior F/A working the first-class cabin shuffled and puffed her way to my seat 1K. Glasses on the tip of her nose and breathing heavily with the exertion of having shuffled 10 ft down the aisle from the galley, she lurched to a stop in front of my seat. Squinting at the seating chart in her hands and obviously hard of hearing, she barked out in a fog-horn like squawk, "MR HARRIS! Wha'da ya wanna EAT?" Not wanting to keep her from spreading her charm around the rest of the FC cabin I smiled up at her and politely replied, "Nothing to eat, thanks, just a glass of champagne". There was a long pause in which her glasses slipped even further down the bridge of her nose and in which, blinking like an owl, she boomed "SALAD?" It was obvious that she hadn't heard me so I said "Champagne!" in a loud but polite tone. When she cupped her ear and bellowed "SALAD?" again I knew that she was most likely deaf as well as blind, so I raised my voice even louder and replied "CHAMPAGNE!"

When she pushed her glasses back up onto her nose and shouted "SALAD?" yet again I was open-mouthed with astonishment. I was about to use my hands as a megaphone to holler back my third and final request for a glass of champagne when the gentleman seated directly across the aisle from me in seat 1A leaned out of his seat, winked at me and shouted, "Just take the DAMN SALAD!" Everyone in the First Class cabin fell about in laughter. When the blind, deaf, inept and sour-faced senior nana shuffled away muttering to herself, I got up from my seat, went into the galley and poured myself a glass of bubbly then dashed back to my seat, swallowed my pill and slept like a baby for the duration of the flight.

I arrived in Melbourne refreshed and ready to experience first-hand the excitement and glamour of Australia's premier sporting event. Like the Kentucky Derby in America, the Melbourne Cup is a grand event, the perfect occasion to dress to the nines and embark upon a day long alcohol imbued party. A highlight of the occasion is Fashions in the Field, in which the best-dressed woman and man are chosen from the spectators.

As Paul had reserved us seats in the member's section, I fully expected to compete with Melbourne's elite. I love any occasion that involves a suit and tie and I was well prepared with two Armani summer-weight suits accessorized with a stylish straw fedora.

Melbourne is famous for being the city with four seasons in one day and Melbourne Cup Day was no exception. When we arrived at Flemington it was hot and humid, a sweltering 38C, and we had already attended a tailgate party outside the racetrack and consumed grilled snags (sausages) as well as several bottles of champagne. By the time it came to place our bets and enter the stands I was sweating like a whore in church. I was trying to place my bet with my jacket slung recklessly over my shoulder, when an official, an elderly man, approached me and drily intoned, "I'm afraid that gentleman are not permitted to remove their jackets while seated in the Members' Box." Furiously fanning myself with my fedora I reluctantly obliged and replaced my suit jacket back over my now sodden shirt.

Studying the racing form before placing my bet, I realized that even though the odds on the horses and jockeys riding them were clearly delineated, I really didn't have a clue as how to pick a winner. When Paul told me that my chances were improved by placing bets on any group of horses to win, place and show, I glanced down at the names of the horses running in the main race and immediately spotted "Champagne"! As the focal point of my trip from Los Angeles concerned champagne, I figured that this was as good an omen as any. To round out my top three picks, I chose Jezebel and another horse whose name I no longer recall. My bets now placed I downed another flute of champagne and joined the excited throng packed into the Members' Box.

It is amazing just how quickly a two-mile horse race can transpire from start to finish. I was on my feet cheering wildly as the race began, but as soon as Paul pointed out that my favorite Champagne was leading the field, I went completely berserk!

In a scene reminiscent of Eliza Doolittle in *My Fair Lady,* I was leaping in the air like a maniac screaming, "Come on Champagne, move your ASS!" As the horses neared the finish line, I was totally out of control, waving my arms in the air, shouting at the top of my lungs for Champagne to, "GO Baby, GO!" Then, at the last furlong, when Jezebel shot seemingly out of nowhere to eclipse Champagne and cross the finish first, I was crestfallen and deflated like a burst balloon. When Paul pointed out that not only had my horse finished in second place but that I had also picked the winner Jezebel and the third place finisher as well, I was ecstatic and was soon surrounded by complete strangers patting me on the back and offering drunken congratulations. After I had calmed down enough to collect my winnings, I discovered that my day at the races had more than paid for my entire holiday and I now had some serious pocket money as well. Needless to say, that evening's drinks were on me!

The next day, fueled by my windfall, Paul took me on an epic shopping excursion to Chapel Street and Melbourne's most eclectic collection of fashionable boutiques. It just happened that major sales were in progress and this was like waving a red flag to a bull and I hit the streets running. Several hours and countless dollars later I was struggling under the weight of my purchases and had acquired so much loot I was forced to buy a larger duffle bag that I had to lug back home as checked luggage.

Paul and his family were fantastic hosts. Paul logged hundreds of kilometers in his car taking me to all of Victoria's main tourist attractions including the incredible natural formations called the Twelve Apostles, the amazing view of the ocean alongside the Great Ocean Road and Phillip Island and its adorable Penguins.

In a whirlwind tour of the city, I was able to take in the National Gallery of Victoria, picnic in the Royal Botanic Gardens, visit the Rod Laver Arena where the Australian Open Tennis Tournament is held, ride the city circle tram and be amazed at the bustling shops on the laneway of Degraves Street.

What resulted in my most outlandish experience was attending my first AFL (Australian Football League) match between Collingwood and Melbourne at the famous Melbourne Cricket Ground, the MCG.

Australians are obsessed with any sporting event and the opportunity to bet on the outcome and since cricket is the national sport the MCG is hallowed ground. The team that Paul follows is Collingwood, so naturally I was also going to support his team. Collingwood's team colors are black with white vertical stripes and players are nicknamed the Magpies after a species of black and white birds.

We were seated in the Collingwood side of the playing field, awash with a crowd of black and white jerseys. In a closely contested match, Collingwood was ahead by 5 points and the rowdy crowd was ecstatic. Paul had taken me down directly behind the goal posts to get active shots as one of the opposing Melbourne players, a strapping 6 ft curly headed blonde, was setting up a kick to take the game. I was busy clicking away with my camera as the player was seconds from kicking the ball when the crowd behind me chanted at the top of their lungs, "ONE, TWO, THREE ... POOOOFTAAAA!" Bug-eyed I almost dropped my camera and turned to Paul and shouted, "What the fuck?" Reveling in my shocked reaction Paul threw back his head roaring with laughter and with tears running down his face said, "Relax mate, they're not calling him out as being gay, they're just messing with him to try and make him miss the post!" I finally closed my mouth when he convinced me that even a crowd of drunken Aussies wouldn't be that *un-PC*!

During the week that I spent with his family, Paul's mother spoiled me with amazing home cooked gourmet meals nightly and as a result I easily gained a few unwanted pounds. The day before I was to return to Los Angeles Paul, who worked as a certified personal trainer, suggested that we do a light walk up the hill. The *hill* turned out to be Mount Dandenong, the highest mountain on the fringes of Melbourne at an elevation of 633 meters (2077 ft)!

When we arrived at the base of Mount Dandenong, I knew that Paul had got the better of me and that I wanted to whine, capitulate and just say, "Oh HELLLL NOO!" Instead, I put on my game face and said, "Screw it, I GOT this, let's DO this!" Even though it was a relatively mild day temperature wise, within an hour or so I was sucking up air and wheezing like old *Puffing Billy*, an antique railway train and tourist attraction that we had passed as it traversed the other side of the Dandenong Ranges.

When another hour had passed, I was seriously entertaining murderous thoughts about the gym Nazi who was torturing me without even breaking a sweat himself! My legs, back and arms had long since turned to jelly but I soldiered on grabbing onto rocks, boulders, branches and stout twigs, ANYTHING that would give me purchase on that damn *hill*! I barely kept up with Paul, who I was now convinced was at least partly the spawn of a mountain goat. I was resolute in my efforts to grin and bear it every time he turned his smiling face to me to ask, "You right there mate?"

We came to a clearing about three quarters of the way to the top and glanced at the television towers that had been our guidepost on the very top of the mountain. Pausing for water and to admire what even I had to admit was a spectacular view of the Melbourne city spread out shimmering in the distance miles below, I felt somewhat exalted from the arduous task of hauling my aching ass up that hill.

It was serenely quiet as Paul pointed out a stone memorial situated in the center of a stand of towering ash trees and dense fern and undergrowth. I walked over to where he was and as if on cue, a beam of sunlight filtered through the thickly forested area and highlighted the plaque on the edifice. I felt an overwhelming sense of sadness when I read that this spot memorialized the crash of an Australian Airways DC2 on October 25, 1938. The Kyeema airliner had crashed into this very spot in heavy fog mistakenly believing that they were headed back to the nearby airport at Essendon. Eighteen people perished at this place and both Paul and I observed several moments of silence in remembrance of the fatal accident. As a direct result of that tragedy, navigational beacons and a 33 MHz radio range system became standardized equipment throughout Australia, providing pilots with accurate information on their flight course.

It was nearing late afternoon when we began our final accent to the top of the mountain. The looming television towers were like a checkered flag or a long distance finish line banner to me and I plodded on exhausted, drenched in grime and sweat like a survivor in a disaster movie to the pavement of the parking lot of the Mount Dandenong Observatory.

I must have looked decidedly out of place when I emerged over the guard rail and stumbled towards the main platform of the observatory; a black man attired in dirt-streaked hiking gear staggering like a runaway slave towards the nearest bar and a much needed *adult beverage*. Paul, on the other hand, appeared as fresh as a daisy, clothing crisp and clean when he thumped me on my back to heartily congratulate me on conquering the hill. I thought that my legs would buckle from the impact and when I had recovered my breath grudgingly agreed that having survived the day long ordeal, it was indeed worth the effort.

We rewarded ourselves with a hearty lunch at the Sky High restaurant, enjoying the spectacular views of the city of Melbourne twinkling in the distance surrounded by its eastern suburbs. I made a valiant attempt to wipe away all my aches and pains with large pints of ice cold Victorian Bitter (VB), one of my favorite beers, while Paul, who annoyingly did not approve of alcoholic beverages due to the supposed negative side effects when bodybuilding, downed a mineral water. After lunch we made good use of the fast fading daylight to head back down the hill, an activity I found infinitely easier than our earlier climb had been on my stiff and aching back, legs and ass. I was ready to weep with relief when we finally spotted Paul's utility vehicle. I gingerly hauled my by now thoroughly exhausted carcass into its luxury and we headed away from the *hill* that had damn near crippled me!

Paul's mum outdid herself preparing a bon voyage feast for my return flight to Los Angeles. It was quite late when the Solomon family finally toasted my health and our enduring friendship. In fact, I have been an official member of the Solomon family ever since that time and a more loving, generous and hospitable group of friends I would be hard pressed to find.

After a magnificent send-off from Paul and his family, I hobbled my agonizingly sore and decrepit body back on to the plane with fond memories of my dear friends, the races, an epic shopping spree and yes, even the *hill*. I settled back into the comfort of my First Class seat and ended my holiday the way it had begun; with a sleeping pill and an ice-cold flute of champagne!

At Brighton Beach in Melbourne

View from Mount Dandenong a.k.a *The Hill*

CHAPTER 35
PARANORMAL ACTIVITY

I have often scoffed at reports of crew members who have experienced supernatural encounters on layovers in hotels that were supposedly haunted by the spirits of entities who had met an untimely end. All of my skepticism vanished however when I found myself confronted with occurrences that neither science nor rational thought could readily explain.

For years, crews had repeated the folklore that our layover hotel in Tahiti had been constructed over the site of an ancient Polynesian burial-ground. One room in particular, the last room on the left-hand side of the hallway on the ground floor facing the ocean, was supposedly haunted by an apparition in a flowing white burial shroud. This unhappy soul was apparently perturbed that its resting place had been disturbed and was determined to drive away anyone who occupied the room. This tale had been repeated on several occasions at drunken crew parties, however by the time we landed in Tahiti, that fact had slipped from my exhausted mind when I was allocated the very room after the flight from LA.

Prior to this particular evening, my only experience with anything even remotely connected to the occult was watching the occasional horror film, a genre of which I have to admit I was not an ardent devotee. In fact, having experienced films like *The Exorcist* and *The Omen* (as opposed to actually watching, since for the most part I peeped through splayed fingers and tightly shut eyes), I avoided anything to do with depictions of demons or hauntings, my own imagination being sufficiently overactive without the aid of gruesome visual images.

With Hazel in Tahiti

It was a bright moonlit night when I finally retired to my room after dinner and drinks with my crew. Taking advantage of the gorgeous view from my lanai, I left the patio door open as well as the drapes in order to catch the breeze and admire the vista of swaying palm fronds and the sound of the ocean breaking on the pristine beach. Prudence and not fear of a recalcitrant ghost compelled me to lock the wire-mesh screen door as a precaution against any unwanted intruders.

My head hit the pillow and within moments, I fell into a deep and dreamless slumber. Around 3am I was jolted awake suddenly conscious of a severe drop in the temperature of my room. I had purposely not turned on the air conditioning, but right now my room was absolutely frigid. As if the bitter cold wasn't enough of a shock to my system, I felt the weight of someone or something pressing down on my chest constricting my ability to breathe. My mind was reeling with fear as I forced my eyes open only to discover pitch-blackness in what had previously been a moonlit room. Now completely terrified I used my elbows to counteract the pressure on my upper body and gasping for air yelled at the top of my lungs, "JESUS!" In that moment the weight shifted and I leapt off the bed and bolted for the door. I flung the door open and, clad only in my underwear, sprinted down the hallway to the room of the nearest crewmember and pounded on her door. I'm certain she was really startled by my appearance and incoherent ranting, but I convinced her to accompany me back to my room to verify that I had not completely lost my mind.

Only a few moments had passed since I flew out of that room leaving the door wide open behind me, but when we approached my room the door was shut, effectively locking us out. We briefly debated calling the front desk to get assistance in re-entering my room, but I had experienced enough bizarre activity for one night and gladly accepted the use of the spare bed in her room, thinking that the warm light of day would reveal a commonplace explanation for what had occurred. I woke shortly after daylight and had the clerk on duty escort me back to my room.

I have always been an obsessively neat person, keeping each hotel room I occupied as organized as possible and although it had been a calm clear night with just a slight breeze, when we opened the door to my room it looked as if a tornado had passed through it. The sheets were on the floor and everything on the desk, including my books and briefcase, was scattered throughout the room.

Amazingly, the screen door was still locked making it impossible for an intruder to have entered from the outside and to have committed this mayhem. The front desk clerk made the sign of the cross and muttered, "MON DIEU!" (MY GOD). I took one look around the space and shouted, "HOLY SHIT!" After hastily retrieving all my belongings, I was allocated a new room for the remainder of my layover, as far as possible from my previously already *occupied* abode, and spent the next night wearing a crucifix, purchased while seriously considering the possibility of an afterlife.

In the early months of 1990 I was on a layover in Sydney, Australia, and along with a flying partner, Joseph D'Amato, we decided to tour the Blue Mountains region located about 50 km west of the city.

We spent the day exploring the Jenolan Caves, then hiking the area around the spectacular Three Sisters, a rock formation close to the town of Katoomba. At sunset, we took a cable car across the site, which afforded us an amazing panoramic view of the valley below.

After dinner and in order to forego the tedium of driving back to the city, we elected to spend the night in an elegant yet derelict-looking hotel that we had noticed earlier in the day. The Hydro Majestic is a grand old edifice originally built in 1904 as a destination for the nearby mineral baths, which were popular at the time. Since this was the off-season as well as before renovation work on both the interior and exterior of the building was to begin, we had the place literally to ourselves apart from a handful of employees. We were given a suite on the second floor in the section that was part of the original structure of the hotel. After touring the main dining room (which was also closed for renovation), we admired our opulent Victorian era accommodation and settled in for the night. Given the age of the building and its appearance I should have immediately characterized this creepy residence as the perfect place for a haunting. The turn-of-the-century decorations, the faded satin wall paper, the floral design of the worn carpeting, the old-fashioned iron radiators and the heavy red and gold brocade curtains adorning large windows offering views of the thickly forested mountains, all combined to create a Gothic atmosphere.

At around 3am I was roused from a deep slumber by a loud and drawn out creaking noise; *CREEEEEEKKKKK!* I had made up my mind to ignore it and immediately shut my eyes as tightly as possible hoping that whatever I had just heard was a figment of my imagination, when an even louder, more menacing *CREEEEEEKKKKK!* began. I shouted across the room to my still comatose traveling companion, "Joe! Wake up! Did you hear that?"

Rousing his head from his pillow, Joe yawned and said, "Yeah. It's probably those old-ass radiators", meanwhile pulling the covers over his head to go back to sleep. No sooner had those words left his mouth than an extremely loud thumping sound began, as if someone in heavy duty boots was stomping about in the room directly above us, rattling both of us to our bones! Since we knew for a fact that we were the ONLY occupants in the entire hotel this immediately had our full and undivided attention. When the CREEEKKING recommenced, now accompanied by the renewed stomping of someone or something directly above us, we simultaneously shouted, "WTF?" Grabbing our overnight bags, we decided that our stay in this joint was definitely OVER! Wild eyed we dashed past a startled night porter and tossing him our keys yelled out, "We're OUT of here!"

It wasn't until we were in the safety of our rental car and headed back to the normalcy of the crowded and specter-free Marriott hotel in Circular Quay that we both looked at each other incredulously and with nervous laughter speculated on just what the hell had been responsible for causing us to flee like frightened schoolgirls into the night.

After that incident, I had several years in which the only spirits I encountered were of the alcoholic variety and I wouldn't be lying if I said that there were more than just a few of those!

I love London in the fall and winter. The city seems to conjure up visions of a Charles Dickens' novel, especially if there is a light drifting of snow on the ground or a chill in the air. Since I had previously lived there for so many years, London was one of my favorite destinations and besides catching up with old friends, I usually spent the 48-hour layover going to my favorite art gallery (either the Tate or Tate Modern), taking in a theatre production in the West End and of course heading to Harrods to stock up on Earl Grey tea.

At that time, our layover hotel in London was the Kensington Garden Hotel directly across the street from Kensington Gardens and Kensington Palace. The hotel itself is a charming example of Edwardian architecture with tall windows offering views of the tree-lined boulevard and a magnificently maintained park. While the exterior and interior of the building had undergone extensive renovations, the hallways were quite long and narrow, twisting and turning at improbable angles creating a veritable labyrinth. The dimly lit passageways and the narrow margins of the space easily contributed to create a spooky atmosphere.

On this particular layover, I had been allocated a room on the top floor of the hotel. The room itself though quite small was cozy and charming, due to the tall garret window with a window seat that looked out onto the park.

It was the last week in November, on a crisp, cold evening when a group of us decided to take the Jack the Ripper and London Ghost Walk. As the daylight faded and darkness descended on the city, five of us huddled together against the cold awaiting our guide for a tour that would follow the trail of the murderous exploits of Jack the Ripper. Since we had fortified our nerves with cocktails earlier in the afternoon, we were in the mood to be enlightened, if not frightened, by visiting the sights of those real life crime scenes from over a century ago. Our guide was dressed in evening entire of the late 1880s embellished with a top hat and evening cape. The gas-lit alleyways and dark corridors of Fleet St, Drury Lane and the notorious East End certainly created a vivid background to the tales of the murderous deeds of one of history's most infamous serial killers.

For over three hours, we were taken to the exact spots where the bodies of five female prostitutes were discovered in the Whitechapel district of London between August 31 and November 9, 1888. Every gory detail of the murders of Mary Ann Nichols, Annie Chapman, Elizabeth Stride, Catherine Eddowes and Mary

Jane Kelly was graphically recounted by our guide, who was fast becoming an expert at scaring us shitless!

By the conclusion of the evening, we were in dire need of a stiff drink to calm our frayed and thoroughly rattled nerves, so we ended the night with several gin and tonics at my favorite pub; The Swan, which was conveniently located a few blocks from our hotel.

Later on and after bidding my crewmembers goodnight, I retired to my attic space and prepared for bed. Seeing that this was a typically cold and damp English night, I was sensibly dressed in flannel pajamas and a cozy, knitted beanie that I used to shut out any unwanted ambient light as well as to keep my head warm. In order to expel the gruesome images of The Ripper's victims from my mind, I decided to read a chapter or two of James Michener's novel *Hawaii*. Propping the pillows up for support, I climbed into bed leaving on the light from the bedside nightstand to illuminate the pages of my thick paperback novel.

I had been thoroughly engrossed in the story unfolding in my book and at least 45 minutes had passed when the drawer of the bedside table holding the lamp slowly slid open about two inches. Noticing movement in my peripheral vision I glanced over, thought to myself, "Hmmmm ...that's odd." I reached over and closed the drawer and continued reading. Ten minutes later the drawer again slid open, wider and slightly faster than before. By now this drawer had my full and undivided attention, so leaping out of bed and turning the rest of the room's lights to full bright, I pulled the draw out from the recesses of the open slot to see if there was a spring or anything which would have caused the drawer to pop open. Satisfied that there was nothing at all in the back of the recalcitrant drawer, I slammed it back into place and for added leverage, propped my roller bag suitcase, which must have weighed 10 lbs, firmly against it. Turning off the main light I climbed back into bed and after reading for another 20 minutes or so decided that I had vanished all thoughts of Jack the Ripper from my head and could now have a sound night's sleep. I was in the process of reaching over to extinguish the lamp on the bedside table when the drawer loudly popped fully open, slamming my suitcase to the floor in the process. My heart was beating wildly as I jumped several feet in the air, meanwhile gurgling out a semi-suppressed scream, "HOLY SHIT...NOT AGAIN!" After scrambling to turn on the main light in the room I gathered my uniform, grabbed my suitcase and bolted down the darkened hallway, racing into the elevator.

I must have made quite a sight to the clerk on duty, disheveled, bug-eyed and in flannel pajamas, rambling on about a ghost or some, "shit that was slamming drawers open and knocking my suitcase on to the floor!" After repeating my story to him more slowly and conceivably more coherently, I convinced him to get me another room, hopefully unoccupied this time, and to have an exorcist check out the room I'd abandoned in a blind panic while he was at it!

Since that last encounter with unwanted guests, I now travel with incense, in particular WHITE SAGE, which even skeptics inform me does wonders to not only freshen the air, but most importantly, keep evil or unhappy spirits at bay.

CHAPTER 36

NEW ZEALAND

Nothing prepared me for the breathtaking natural beauty of New Zealand. I had often heard the old saw; "New Zealand... a country of four million, three quarters of which are SHEEP!" What these cynics had failed to mention was the sheer jaw-dropping beauty of the place.

In the late 1990s and into the first half of 2000, we enjoyed eight-day trips to Auckland, a long layover broken up only by a shuttle flight of three hours and 15 minutes to Sydney, Australia, landing back in Auckland in time for dinner, or in my case, just-in-time to hit the nightclubs conveniently located on Queen St, within easy walking distance from our hotel. The lengthy layovers gave us ample opportunity to thoroughly enjoy Auckland and to explore the surrounding places of interest. Situated in a natural bay and surrounded by water and incredible views, Auckland quickly became one of my favourite destinations. The hospitality and innate friendliness of the inhabitants (indeed of those of the entire country) only enhanced Auckland's natural beauty.

Located in the centre of the city itself was the Sky Tower, which at 328 m or 1076 ft was the tallest freestanding structure in the southern hemisphere. This observation and telecommunications tower, besides being an architectural marvel, was crowned by the Orbit revolving restaurant, which not only served superb cuisine but offered amazing views of the surrounding countryside up to 82 km away.

A favourite with our crews was a visit to Rotorua, famed for its numerous natural hot springs and geysers located throughout the city. After a 12 hr and 35 min flight from Los Angeles, nothing compared to indulging in a bottle or two of New Zealand's lauded wines while soaking our aching limbs in one of the many natural hot springs. Due to the effects of several bottles of wine, as well as the increasingly hot temperatures of the water, inhibitions were lowered and more often than not bathing suits magically disappeared lending the air of a Bacchanalia to the proceedings. Lest I leave you with any salacious implications, I can assure you that nothing untoward occurred, and in any case we were all too well acquainted with each other for any lusty activities to occur!

The food in Auckland was always fresh, plentiful and delicious. We often prepared large picnic hampers loaded with local delicacies and chilled white wine and headed to Abel National Park at the northern tip of the South Island. Cars are not allowed in the park itself but the long drive to get there was well worth the effort. When we arrived, we encountered a spectacular beach leading to many challenging hiking trails offering breathtaking views of the amazing scenery that surrounded you in every direction.

My favourite destinations included one of the most beautiful places that I have ever laid eyes on, The Bay of Islands, which contained 144 islands, each with secluded beaches. On any given day, you could indulge in whale and dolphin spotting as well as observing penguins, all in their natural habitat. The place is a nature lover's dream and nothing short of paradise. The same could be said of Milford Sound, which is located on the South Island at the northern end of Fiordland National Park. Milford Sound is surrounded by the most ruggedly beautiful coastal scenery imaginable and even the most amateur photographer, by pointing a camera in any direction, could capture a shot of picture-postcard perfection.

As reckless and foolhardy as I was in those now distant years, when I was convinced that I could do anything and that nothing could harm me, there was one crew activity in which I absolutely refused to participate. Whenever the subject of Bungy Jumping came up I was invariably the sole voice of reason, explaining in no uncertain terms the sheer stupidity of strapping a rubber band around my ankles (no matter how thick or secure a band) and leaping into a yawning abyss with nothing below to cushion the impact but roiling and turbulent water!

Auckland Harbour Bridge was the preferred spot for this act of lunacy and, at 43 m above the water flowing below, no amount of cajolery (or alcohol for that matter) would suffice to convince me to take that *leap of faith*. Just peering over the side of the bridge was quite enough to satisfy any dare-devil tendencies I may have drunkenly harboured and was in fact an instantaneous way to sober up! Visiting the casino (even though my chances of cashing in at the gaming tables was on a par with picking the winning Lotto numbers) or dancing the night away in one of the many clubs on Queen Street was more to my liking.

By far and away the most memorable occurrence on my Auckland layovers was making the acquaintance of one of Auckland's major movers and shakers; Amy Miller. By the happiest of circumstance, The Silk Gallery, an up-scale boutique located in our layover hotel, the Sheraton, was owned by Amy. For an inveterate shopaholic like myself, it wasn't long before I wandered into her emporium and was captivated by the vast array of bold silk fabrics and brass and wooden furnishings that would not have been out of place in either a palace or Aladdin's fabled den. I was deeply engrossed in admiring these treasures when a voice from behind me musically inquired, "Good afternoon, may I be of any assistance?" I turned around and standing before me was one of the most beautiful, most stylishly dressed woman I had ever laid eyes on. Amy Miller was and still is stunning, in every sense of the word. Of Fijian-Indian descent, her raven coloured hair, cut in a smart bob and wearing a salmon coloured Chanel suit, a double strand of black Tahitian pearls and black patent leather Jimmy Choo sling-back stilettos, Amy would have given Anna Wintour (editor of Vogue magazine) a run for her money in the fashion stakes! A natural and spontaneous warmth radiated from her eyes and ready smile and from that instant on we were comrades in arms and devoted friends.

Due to Amy's connections, I was granted an all-access pass into the BEST restaurants, nightspots and parties in Auckland. The America's Cup yacht race was being contested in New Zealand that year and through Amy I found myself invited to some of the wildest, most alcohol-infused dusk-till-dawn parties I have ever attended. My somewhat groggy afternoons were spent either sailing in Auckland's magnificent harbour or enjoying champagne picnics or brunches with Amy in the fashionable suburb where she resided, Ponsonby. It was in Amy's company at an art gallery opening in Vulcan Lane that I spent a pleasurable half hour discussing modern art with an extremely articulate and knowledgeable woman who had introduced herself as Helen, when suddenly a pair of burly bodyguards approached her and quietly pointed out that, "It's time to go Prime Minister". My mouth fell open; the art scholar I had been chanting with was none other than New Zealand Prime Minister Helen Clark, quite heady stuff for a boy from Wisconsin!

Amy befriended several F/As and became our resident tour guide, social arbiter and den mother all rolled into one delightful package. Her home became our de-facto layover residence and was the scene of numerous outrageous soirees. I recall one boisterous night in particular when fuelled by far too much alcohol and joints, I donned one of Amy's fur wraps and performed *Falling in Love Again* (a song made famous by Marlene Dietrich in the 1930 film *Blue Angel*) in both English & mangled German. Amid howls of laughter from my drunken crew, I ended up sprawled, flat on my face drunk as a skunk and oblivious to the world. Somewhere, someplace there must be a manual on how to regain and retain your dignity after waking up face down and drooling on a carpet! The only saving factor in this scenario was that the rest of my crew awoke in far worse condition than I did.

The Lord of the Rings was being filmed in New Zealand at this time and on several occasions I had the privilege and pleasure of ferrying several of the main actors in the movie between LA and Auckland. Because of the frequency of my trips between both cities, I became quite friendly with Elijah Wood who played Frodo Baggins and Sir

Ian Mckellen who immortalized Gandalf the Grey, the wise wizard and main stay in the trilogy. Both of these men were charming and delightful people to keep company with, making what could have been a tedious journey pass quickly and effortlessly by. As a matter of fact, Elijah became so comfortable after a few drinks that he ended up displaying an elfish rune tattoo placed prominently on his hipbone! The entire cast had these matching tattoos to commemorate both the experience and camaraderie of the time spent together on set making the film.

Both the television series *Xena: Warrior Princess* and *Hercules* were also filmed in New Zealand and even though I had Kevin Sorbo (Hercules) on numerous trips, I never had the pleasure of meeting Lucy Lawless, the star of *Xena*. I would have given my eye-teeth to come face-to-face with Ms Lawless as I was not only an ardent fan of hers, but I harboured fantasies of joining her in yelling her war cry of, "AIE! AIE! AIE! AIE!" full throttle in the galley!

I was working the shuttle flight between Sydney and Auckland with Kathleen Calogne, a close friend of many years, whose birthday we were planning on celebrating that night at a venue on Queen St. An avid sport fan, I was thrilled when we noticed that several members of New Zealand's All Blacks rugby team were travelling with us on our return flight to Auckland. Kathleen, a native of New Orleans and a GSLQ (Grand Southern Lady of Quality), was demurely admiring these specimens of athletic perfection from the opposite end of the drink trolley we were pushing up the aisle, when, striking up a conversation with the footballer seated in the aisle seat, I asked what position he played. When he responded he was a *hooker*, I tried my damnedest to keep a poker face while arching my eyebrows and innocently replying, "Reeeaaaalllly? Since its Kathleen's birthday and I only have $100 cash on me, could you make an exception and …. take a credit card?" There was a split second hesitation while his eyes widened followed immediately by uproarious laughter from not only the *hooker* in question but all of his mates seated in the immediate vicinity. When the hilarious commotion subsided, he gave me a wide smile and a knowing wink and replied, "Cheeky bastard, I will see what I can do!" Kathleen, whose complexion had finally returned to its normal colour (as opposed to the flaming crimson it had taken on during this exchange), blew our *Happy Hooker* an air kiss and smirking and chuckling to ourselves we continued on down the aisle.

At one point, our hotel was undergoing extensive renovations and for a short period of time we were relegated to a small motel abutting a dairy farm. As Amy was on a shopping expedition to Europe and India for fabrics and artefacts for her store, we were left for a time to our own devices, which usually involved drinking ourselves into a stupor. With virtually nothing to do but count cow patties, I'm embarrassed to recount that on more than one occasion, as puerile and juvenile as it sounds, cow tipping was the evening's main event.

One evening, however, long after we had all retired to our respective rooms that were all located on the ground floor of the motel, we were startled awake from a deep slumber by a bloodcurdling scream. Rushing into the hallway, we encountered one of the more senior crewmembers wearing curlers and a floor length flannel nightgown shrieking that there was a Peeping Tom lurking outside her window. Rushing past our shaken comrade, we came crashing to a halt. There looming large in the window was the placid face of a cow, which had obviously wandered from her nearby pasture. After falling against each other howling with laughter, we assured our co-worker that the perpetrator was completely harmless, and drawing the curtains securely closed, we tucked our thoroughly embarrassed co-worker into bed and bid her a safe and sound goodnight.

Beyond doubt my most adventurous and memorable birthday to date occurred in the South Island of New Zealand. For eight days, a group of eight of my closest friends from both Australia and New Zealand spent an incredible time touring Queenstown on the shore of Lake Wakatipu. Since my birthday is in July (being winter in the Southern Hemisphere) the highlight of my trip was helicopter skiing in The Remarkables in the Southern Alps. Every day was magnificent and the scenery from the mountain heights defied description.

Even though I was raised in the frigid winters of Wisconsin, nothing prepared me for the bitterly cold blast of bone chilling air that arrived from the depths of Antarctica, a type of cold that even three layers of thermal silk underwear and a down parker could not dispel. I honestly don't think I thawed out completely during the entire time we spent in Queenstown, but it was by far the best birthday of my life. Ironically on the night we celebrated my birthday, shivering with the cold and contemplating the possibility of frostbite on my extremities, I was presented with a colourful cake made of ice cream and blazing with candles!

Near the end of 2000, UAL announced that it was pulling out of the New Zealand market, ceding a direct service from LAX to Auckland to our Star Alliance partner Air New Zealand. This move was as unexpected as it was heartbreaking to our flight crews. The only mitigating factor in this depressing scenario was that even though we would no longer have intimate contact with the many friends we had made over the years in New Zealand, neither distance nor time could dim the endearing and everlasting bonds we had forged with its incredibly warm and wonderful people.

Skiing the Remarkables in Queenstown

CHAPTER 37
CREEPY CRAWLIES

The continent of Australia has a well-deserved reputation for containing some of the world's deadliest critters. If they can creep, crawl, bite or swim, there is a damn good likelihood of your experiencing a painful and protracted demise after coming into contact with any of them. While not every creature is deadly or will cause you harm, some by their very appearance can put the fear of God into you!

I was on my hands and needs crawling around the carpet of my hotel room and cursing under my breath, searching for a misplaced shoe. Since I was on the top floor of the Hilton in Sydney, a luxury hotel, I had absolutely no reason whatsoever to expect to encounter anything out of the ordinary. The hotel room was appointed with floor-to-ceiling windows, however, which could be cranked open a few inches for ventilation. At the exact moment I spotted my shoe underneath the desk and was crawling head down ass up in the air, I spotted in my peripheral vision what I could only think was the biggest, ugliest, hairiest TARANTULA I had ever seen!

Knocking my head against the bottom of the desk with a loud THUNK and screaming at the top of my lungs, I backed my ass as quickly as possible out from under the desk, and grabbing the phone yelled out, "Get somebody up here IMMEDIATELY....there is a HUGE TARANTULA in my room!" I was cowering near the front door of my room which was now wide open, as I had no intention of being in the same space as a monstrous, possibly poisonous arachnoid, when two bellmen came trotting out of the elevator and headed for my room. Shaking with fear, I directed them to the spot underneath the desk where I had last seen the creature lurking. My mouth was agog when, after capturing the spider and flicking it out of the open window, they laughingly told me, "Mate that was a HUNTSMAN spider. It's completely harmless." Frowning, I frostily replied, "Harmless or not, that UGLY bastard scared the living SHIT out of me." Furthermore, I added, they had better make certain he didn't leave any *relatives* behind to disturb my rest.

One of the many perks of my job was the availability of discounted air travel on other carriers. When in Sydney, I often took advantage of that fact to treat myself and a companion to flying 41 km north of the city to Palm Beach, one of the jewels of Sydney's northern beaches. The best part about this adventure was taking a seaplane from Rose Bay, a short distance from our hotel, and flying along the gorgeous coastline for a half hour or so and landing near Barrenjoey Lighthouse.

Notwithstanding the magic carpet views that passed beneath us, Palm Beach (as well as neighbouring Whale Beach and Avalon to the south) was the perfect spot to while away an entire day. We would swim in the turquoise colored waters of the ocean, have a leisurely snack and then hike to the still operational lighthouse which was constructed in 1881. Climbing down from the lighthouse, we would enjoy a delicious seafood lunch of chilled prawns and lobster tails, all washed down with champagne. One time while truly satiated, I was strolling along the shoreline idly immersing my feet in the rock pools that dotted the shoreline, when I noticed what I took to be a quite remarkable and striking yellow starfish with vivid bright blue markings. I bent directly over the starfish and was mere inches from picking it up for a closer inspection, when a man in his mid-30s walking with his young son next to him yelled out, "MATE! DONT TOUCH THAT!" Jumping back in alarm I asked, "Why not.... what's wrong?" He proceeded to inform me that what I had taken to be a harmless starfish was in fact a Blue-Ringed Octopus, one of the most DEADLY creatures in the sea. Even though the thing was no more than five inches in diameter at best, I was told that its venom was strong enough to KILL me within minutes! Apparently, it secretes a toxin that is 200 times more powerful than cyanide and you end up dying from motor paralysis and cardiac arrest due to lack of oxygen.

By now thoroughly petrified I was further warned that this particular critter lived in the shallows of tidal pools in which I was trailing my bare feet, a bit of information that I took to heart and that made me bust a move to get onto the sand and relatively dry land as quickly as my shaking legs would carry me! Needless to say, from that day onward, I kept a wary eye on the shoreline, particularly rock pools, whenever I ventured into the ocean.

CHAPTER 38

MORE SHIT THAT CRAWLS

While on a layover in Melbourne, Australia, I made the acquaintance of Craig Waters, a resident of Beaudesert, a small town located some 91 km (57mi) south of Brisbane in the Scenic Rim Region of Queensland. Craig was in Melbourne to stock-up on supplies for his homestead, a 2600 ha sprawling property nestled in the rolling hills and extensive woodland of that area.

Although I had travelled extensively in New South Wales, I had never visited Queensland, so when Craig invited me to spend time on his property, I happily accepted. I didn't know it at the time, but I was about to gain a first-hand knowledge of and personal experience with a few of Australia's nastiest creatures.

To get to Beaudesert, I had to first fly into Brisbane near Australia's famed Gold Coast. Craig collected me from the airport in his sturdy white four-wheeled drive Toyota Land Cruiser for the hour or so trip to Beaudesert. The drive southwest was breathtaking as we travelled past mountainous terrain and rolling verdant horse farms.

We finally reached a bend in the main highway passing beneath a large wooden archway that straddled two thick, ancient gum trees with the name Cressdale carved into it. I figured that we had at last reached his home. However, this turned out to be the main thoroughfare that after a drive of 25 minutes led to the actual house itself; a large, spectacular, wooden-framed Queenslander (a home built on a raised platform for climate reasons), surrounded by a magnificent veranda attached to three sides of the main building.

It took very little imagination on my part to envision that I had arrived on the set of *The Thorn Birds*, a favorite film of mine. I was gob-smacked, busily admiring the beauty and the architectural perfection of the structure, when Val Waters, Craig's 60-year-old grandmother bounded down the steps from the porch and enveloped me in a warm welcoming embrace. "Nan" as I was instructed to address her and Craig ran the property on their own, overseeing a large herd of cattle, countless sheep, horses, pigs and *chooks* as well as maintaining all 2600 ha of land that had been in their family for generations. The main house had been first constructed in the late 1880s and had been added to and improved upon throughout the years. In its present state it contained a wide, airy sitting room, four elegant bedrooms, spacious kitchen and eating area, a glass enclosed mudroom/bath and a laundry.

For me, however, the piece de resistance was an enormous library located in the center of the building, lined on all four walls with floor-to-ceiling books. Like myself, Nan was a voracious reader and the collection in her library was as extensive and varied as it was impressive. With the dawn till dusk schedule of their average workday, Nan loved nothing better than to unwind on the veranda off her bedroom and relax with a good read. We bonded instantaneously, sharing opinions about our favorite authors and novels that had made an impact on us.

Cressdale property

After a mid-day meal worthy of a king, every course of which was home grown and supplied by their own livestock, Craig took me on a quick tour of the area immediately surrounding the house. Our mode of transportation were the *quad* or *four-wheeler* motorbikes that, when in work mode, were used to round up cattle or corral horses, but were great fun to cruise around at break-neck speed through the nearby hills and valleys.

As this was a working property and not a dude ranch, both Craig and Nan retired early in the evening to bed after an equally delicious but less elaborate dinner, and since I was on holiday, left me to my own devices. Selecting an aged, leather-bound copy of Alexander Dumas' *Count of Monte Cristo* from the library, I strolled onto the veranda adjacent to my bedroom, which was gorgeously appointed with family heirlooms, and settled into a king-sized four-poster bed to read until jet-lag and sleep overcame me. When I was alone, two things were glaringly apparent. The first of these was that there was absolutely no ambient light save for the light emanating from my room; the second was that the area directly outside and in front of me was an all-enveloping and total darkness so indecipherable and complete that for a scant moment I thought I had gone blind! As it was a clear, moonless night it wasn't until I looked up at the sky in awe and amazement that I realized that never in my life had I seen so many stars... so many constellations!

Engrossed as I was in admiring the canopy of an incomprehensible number of planets above and seemingly all around me, it took a moment for another anomaly to strike me; I was engulfed in an absolute total quiet. Not one siren, passing automobile or the omni-present helicopters of Los Angeles penetrated this country haven. I was immediately aware of the sounds of nature and quite honestly it SCARED the SHIT out of me! Every murmur of distant animals, every bird or insect movement was amplified a million fold and in my mind the noise was transformed into a beast of prey, or worse, lurking in the pitch-darkness to devour me!

Putting such ridiculous thoughts out of my head I silently laughed at my city-bred foolishness and after crawling into bed fell into a deep and dreamless slumber.

I was awakened at dawn's crack, quite literally, by the voice of Nan yelling, "Craig, SNAKE. GET the GUN!" This was followed immediately by the sharp and unmistakable crack of a gunshot. Bolting out of bed at breakneck speed and heading to where I could hear Craig shout, "GOT IT NAN!" I was shaking with fright as I observed Craig and Nan in the doorway of the laundry room standing over what was left of a very large, dun-colored four to five foot snake. Finally noticing me quivering on tip-toe looking over their shoulders, Craig nonchalantly intoned, "Brown Snake mate, deadly poisonous!" The wide-eyed and terrified look on my face must have spoken volumes as seconds later they both chuckled and Nan told me, "Not to worry, they can't get at ya when they're DEAD!" Day ONE and I'd already encountered a slithering creature right out of my nightmares! I spent that morning at breakfast with my legs tucked underneath me, ready to flee at a moment's notice.

That morning, Craig took me on an extended hike of the area surrounding the homestead. We climbed a steep ridge, which offered a bird's-eye view of the sprawling property that encompassed the distant horizon as far as the naked eye could see. The heavily forested landscape included several picturesque streams and ponds and it was while crossing one of these creeks that I encountered one of the strangest animals I'd ever laid eyes on. With a fur-covered body and tail that at first glance I had taken to belong to a beaver, but with a bill like that of a duck, it was a platypus, one of nature's oddest creatures. Just as I was about to move in for a closer inspection of this seemingly harmless creature, Craig informed me that its hind legs contained a venomous spur that would most likely cause an un-pleasant reaction if I managed to get scratched. In what must have been a record of some sort I had encountered two potentially deadly and poisonous critters, both before lunch!

Before setting out on our trek, even though I was sensibly dressed in jeans, thick socks and sturdy hiking boots, I asked Craig just what would happen should I suffer the misfortune of being bitten by a snake or spider or any of the myriad creatures that lurked about the property. The answer to my query, "No worries mate The Flying Doctor could get here in no time" did little to banish my qualms about *going WALKABOUT in the BUSH,* given A: the lack of or at best poor cell phone reception in the area and B: the amount of time it would take for the aforementioned doctor to fly in to my rescue! In my mind's eye, I could picture the headlines in one of the more lurid tabloids; "Man dies AGONIZING death after being bitten by... (fill in the blank: SPIDER, SNAKE) while on Holiday Walkabout."

The next few days were as peaceful and idyllic as any I have ever experienced. I soon settled into a routine of retiring to bed earlier than I had done since childhood (8-9 pm) and arising at the crack of dawn (for ME anyway at 6am!) to join Nan and Craig as they went about feeding and herding cattle and horses, collecting eggs from the hen-house and feeding the pigs and sheep. I was always wary of entering the barn as I had been warned to watch-out for *Petey*, a five-feet-long carpet python that lived in the rafters. While I was assured that this type of snake was harmless, subsisting on rats and other vermin, I was terrified of looking up to find a BIG-ASS SNAKE coiled directly over my head!

I have to admit that while I quite enjoyed the physical aspect of working on the property, I harboured absolutely no illusion that I would ever become a bonafide Aussie cowboy. This was purely a working holiday and I was far too steeped in the lifestyle of an *urban sophisticate*, drinking, shopping and partying, to ever *go bush!*

It was while walking under one of the indigenous gum trees in the forest abutting the house that I fell victim to one of the oldest ruses in Oz. Craig who had been walking directly in front of me suddenly stopped stock-still and whispered, "Mate, don't move or look up suddenly. There's a DROP BEAR directly over your head!" Taking his warning to heart, I froze in place, then SLOWLY I looked up to where he was pointing squeaked out hoarsely, "What ....what is a Drop Bear?" Craig replied, "Well, it's a lot like a Koala bear only extremely vicious. They drop down from the branches in the trees and BITE you in the neck!"

Now horrified, I was debating whether or not to bolt from my vulnerable position under the trees when Craig literally fell to the ground laughing. When he could breathe again he told me that not only were such creatures non-existent but they were a folk-tale used to frighten children and un-wary yokels like me! Realizing that I had been pranked, I chucked a rock in his general vicinity and soon joined him in laughing over his *gotcha* moment.

The nine days that I spent at Cressdale were a complete departure from the hectic and fast paced trials and tribulations of everyday life in Los Angeles. I completely detoxed from the stress of living in a bustling, crowded and noisy metropolis and instead found a great appreciation for the calm tranquillity of being enveloped in the natural beauty of the mountains and forests of Queensland.

Where I had previously only considered the coastal areas of Australia with its stunning beaches and ocean views; my version of Paradise, I soon came to consider Beaudesert and the area surrounding it as a Garden of Eden. I immersed myself in country life, attending a fancy-dress (or costume) Bush Dance, having a blast while learning to line dance and tossing back a few stiff drinks with the locals. As a matter of fact, the only drawback I could find with living on such a vast property was the length of time it took to drive to neighbouring spots to socialize or participate in any activity that wasn't readily accessible.

On one memorable occasion Craig drove us nearly two hours from Cressdale to attend a movie that was being held in the town hall of Josephville. The movie was called *Sons of Matthew*, a black and white Australian film made in 1947, which was filmed on location in Queensland. The film was notable for the fact that is was made in extremely adverse conditions (near constant torrential rain) and told the story of Irishman Matthew O'Riordan and his English wife Jane, pioneers of the Lamington Plateau in South Eastern Queensland and the near super-human efforts they undertook to forage a homestead in the area. As an African-American tourist who wanted to learn as much as possible about the area, the film was fascinating to me. Apparently, the film itself was not quite as fascinating as I was from the attention I received upon entering the hall where the film was to be screened. Several rows of seats had been set up in front of a large screen in the very front of the room and as Craig and I made our way into the venue, a hush fell over the room that had been buzzing with conversation moments before. Literally every head snapped back to GAWK at the sole dark face in a sea of lily-white patrons, although admittedly there were a FEW sun-bronzed bodies. Even in a small country town, I'd wager that these folks must have assuredly come across some Aboriginal persons (who after all were the ORIGINAL settlers of the country, at some point in their lives). My assumption was perhaps because of my snappy attire (a blue/ green Ralph Lauren polo shirt paired with khaki chinos and Sperry Topsiders) and NOT my complexion that I must have been the first BLACK AMERICAN they had ever seen outside of a TV screen.

After what seemed an eternity to me but in fact was probably seconds, Craig noisily cleared his throat and with a noise like chalk scrapping a blackboard, pulled back our metal folding chairs before we plopped ourselves down in our seats which were located three quarters of the distance from the screen. The novelty of my presence subsided because as the lights dimmed and the film flickered over the screen the audience's attention shifted from me to the film itself. That is the attention of everyone with the exception of a seven-year-old girl who was seated directly in front of me, and who with her mouth agape could not stop fixing me with a look of consternation and perplexity. Finally, after putting up with her unblinking, unwavering stare for a full five minutes, I made the scariest face I could muster and sticking out my tongue and barring my teeth, not only scared the hell out of her but caused her to jump out of her seat, and hurriedly facing the screen again, nestle as close as she could to the safety of her mother's arms.

The rest of the evening passed without incident.

Sons of Matthew served as a tutorial of sorts for me as we set out for Lambert National Park, where we planned on camping and spending a few evenings at O'Reilly's Rainforest Retreat, which was located in the heart of the park itself. I do not necessarily suffer from a fear of heights, my workplace is after all located at 39,000 ft above the horizon, but the winding, zig-zagging drive up the mountain to get to O'Reilly's left me in a vertiginous state, drenched in sweat. The retreat is well known for its rainforest location and unique and diverse wildlife as well the home of Australian bushman, Bernard O'Reilly, who located the survivors of the 1937 Stinson plane crash. Craig and I were joined by Sarah, a close friend of his, and the three of us set out hiking (or bush walking) through the numerous trails located in the steep, densely wooded terrain. The high point of that first day for me was trekking along the Tree Top Walk, a 180 m long suspension bridge perched 20 m above the rain forest floor. The experience was a delightful one and the views of the McPherson Range were breathtaking. For a while I began to think that I was way out of my league as I attempted to keep pace with Craig and Sarah as we hiked through steep terrain and brambles to the actual site of the Stinson plane crash. I had formed a great admiration for Bernard O'Reilly for the incredible stamina and fortitude it must have taken for him to traverse this steep, densely forested area to come to the aid of the three survivors of that calamity.

On the way back down the mountain we paused to take in the Scenic Rim Bird Sanctuary, where I hand fed Crimson Rosella's and King Parrots, which were not only incredibly bold but beautiful as well. We ended that first day by taking the Flying Fox Zip-Line, a 165-ft long adrenaline-pumping ride through the tops of the rainforest. It was an exhilarating end to a thoroughly exhausting but exciting day.

After two days of luxuriating in the O'Reilly Lodge we set out for the camping grounds near Binna Burra. While the area surrounding the campsite was an idyllic paradise, it was in this particular Garden of Eden that I came face to face with my Bête Noir.

CHAPTER 39
ONCE BITTEN TWICE SHY

After a delicious meal prepared by Craig (who proved to be an excellent chef) and a peaceful night sleeping under a canopy of brilliant stars, we awoke at dawn to prepare for the day's activities. We spent the first day enjoying hiking along several of many trails within the park and I experienced some of the most beautiful rugged terrain I had ever seen. At midday we paused to swim in a crystal clear and very deep pond that was fed from a cascading waterfall. After a morning spent scurrying over rocks, dunking underneath fallen branches and climbing steep inclines, we found this swimming hole to be total bliss. We spent the better part of the afternoon relaxing and enjoying our lunch at the edge of the waterfall, sunbathing and storing up our energy for the long hike back to our camp. Some of the photos I captured of that secluded paradise would have made Ansel Adams proud!

I was trudging along just behind Sarah who was about 6 feet ahead of me when Craig in a steady but firm voice called out, "Tal....mate don't move!" Instantly freezing in place I glanced back at Craig and in my peripheral vision saw something long, shiny and black slither past where I had been standing only moments before. As the creature slithered into the dry, dead brush, I caught a glimpse of colour, dark red, just before I lost sight of it. When my bowels had un-clenched and I could speak again I blurted out, "What ...the fuck ...was that?" Craig, who had drawn next to me but kept his eyes on the ground where I had last spotted movement, quietly replied, "Oh yeah mate, that was a red-bellied black snake." As my eyes widened in horror he added, "Yep... deadly poisonous. Good thing you didn't move!" This titbit of information completely changed my demeanour and I spent the rest of the hike back to the campsite with my shoulders tensely hunched and my eyes peeled to the ground, ready to flee at a moment's notice.

Whereas before I had been blissfully enjoying nature, my attention was now firmly focused on the sobering fact that this *Garden of Eden* was teeming with shit that can kill you! I didn't fully relax until later that evening when I had a full belly and more than a few cold beers to bolster my rapidly diminishing courage.

The next day, we once again awoke at the first signs of daylight and after a hearty breakfast set about preparing for the most challenging adventure of our trip. Both Sarah and Craig were experienced rock climbers and had selected a relatively easy 90 m vertical cliff face in the Binna Burra mountain range for my introduction to the sport. All of the hiking and trekking of the previous three days over rough terrain had definitely increased my stamina and the muscles in my legs, so I was quite eager to give it a try.

After a 45 minute trek through the bush, we arrived at the face of the mountain and the site Craig had selected for my maiden climb. Glancing up at the near vertical rock face I have to admit that I felt a momentary apprehension, but with solid assurances from both my companions that appearances were deceiving and this spot wasn't that difficult, I banished my qualms and assured myself, "You can do this!" Being the novice climber in the group, I was tethered to both Craig and Sarah by a sturdy, yet thinly coiled rope, leaving about 10 feet between us. With Craig in the lead and the admonition to, "not let go...whatever you do!" we began our ascent. We had changed into more suitable footwear for the climb (I had borrowed a pair of climbing shoes from Craig) that made it easier to get a toe-hold on the rock surface, and we each carried a small bag of chalk attached around our waist in order to keep our hands dry and to maintain a stronger grip on the rock. I kept my eyes peeled on Craig's every movement above me, placing my hands and feet in the exact places in which he had gained leverage. With shouts of encouragement from both above and below me, I made a steady if at times awkward ascent up the rock face. When Craig reached the top and peering down asked me, "You alright there mate?" I grinned and grunted up at him, "Oh yeah.... I got this!" I was less than five feet from the top when I spotted a fairly large shelf in the rock above me and slightly to the left of where Craig had climbed, and figuring this appeared to be an easier route, placed my right hand in a crevice and began to pull myself up. Two things occurred simultaneously: I thought to myself, "Damn ...but this rock is squishy" and I pulled myself upwards and onto the protruding rock-shelf. The second that my shoulders had cleared the area I came face to face with the ugliest, most vicious looking reptile I had ever laid eyes on! The *squishy rock* turned out to be a grey and brown colored lizard, whose huge head and unblinking eyes now locked on to mine. Before I could redistribute my weight and get away from this three-ft-long monster (which had an equally long tail), it sank its sharp teeth and claws into the flesh underneath my left armpit. On impulse I let out a yell that must have been audible for miles as I scrambled to get on the ledge and screamed, "Get this creature off me ASAP!" Craig, who had been anxiously watching from just above me, tightened his grip on the rope and shouted, "Tal don't let go!" By now I had reached a spot where I could manoeuvre myself into a more secure position all the while bashing the still thrashing lizard against the rock next to me and crying out, "Get the fuck off me!"

I finally succeeded in separating the lizard from my body, and kicking out with my left foot, flung the creature away from me, sending it careening down the face of the cliff. While keeping a death-grip on the now taunt rope that attached me to Craig, I snuck a glance down at Sarah below me and she shouted out, "It's okay...it didn't fall on me!" Forcing myself to concentrate and with an adrenaline rush that calmed my nerves, I managed to climb the last five feet up the cliff and with Craig giving me a strong-armed assist, clambered over the top collapsing in a heap at his feet. Sarah scrambled up mere minutes later gasping, "Jesus ...are you alright?" It was only when I had stopped shaking and could catch my breath that I noticed my torn tee shirt and blood seeping out where the lizard's teeth had pierced my skin. After examining my wound and assuring me that I wasn't in imminent danger of dying,

Craig hauled me to my feet, stating that we would be taking the fastest route down (a hiking trail), rinsed my wound with water and said that we would get it properly attended to ASAP. When my knees had stopped shaking and I regained my breath if not my composure, I leaned as far over the cliff as I dared and yelled, "You ...mother fucker! I hope I find your ass ...and turn you into a pair of boots!"

After coming to the conclusion that I had experienced more than enough excitement for the week, we decided to cut my excursion short and made our way back down the mountain. After washing out my wound once again and wrapping it with a torn, clean tee shirt, we packed up our campsite. We made a detour on the way back to Cressdale, stopping at a pharmacy we had noticed on the way into the park. After we had explained what had happened the pharmacist supplied us with an antibiotic ointment and surgical dressing. From the size and diameter of the bite marks, both the pharmacist and Craig speculated the *beast* was most likely a lace monitor lizard, which I had interrupted sunning itself on the rock ledge. While he didn't think my wound was life threatening, the pharmacist advised me to see a doctor as soon as possible. With this admonition ringing in my ears I decided to curtail the remainder of my holiday and head back to LA, and my personal physician, the very next day.

After assuring my hosts that I had indeed had a wonderful time immersing myself in country life, it was high time I headed back to the hustle and bustle (and relative safety) of LA, where it was highly unlikely that I'd fall victim to a monstrous lizard anytime soon.

Twenty-four hours later, as I was settled into my FC seat nursing my tightly-bandaged wound - with a double vodka on the rocks - I had to concede to myself that all things considered I'd had an extremely exciting, adventurous holiday. And to this day, I still have the half-moon scars on my upper-left rib cage to prove it!

CHAPTER 40

A CASE OF MISTAKEN IDENTITY

At some point in our lives, we have all been told that we resemble another person or that we have certain personality traits that remind them of a close associate or friend. While it has been pointed out to me on more than one occasion that I look or act remarkably like someone else, I will never forget an incident in which my surname resulted in a case of mistaken identity.

On a flight from LA to Sydney, I had the privilege of serving Patti LaBelle, one of the world's preeminent singers of Rhythm and Blues, an icon of Soul music, as well as an accomplished author and actress. Her buoyant, vivacious personality permeated the entire First Class cabin, turning a routine 15-hour flight into a non-stop party. Miss LaBelle completely turned the tables on the working crew making us feel as if we were the guests of honour in her living room. In a short period of time we were on a first-name basis with this diva and at one point she even had our staid, straight-laced captain dancing in the aisles. I can state with absolute certainty that this particular flight was without doubt the most fun I have ever had while working in my entire career. The entire first FC cabin and half of business class were occupied by Miss LaBelle's entourage as well as by music executives from her recording label (at that time MCA Records).

Our crew was delighted to discover that Patti was not only staying in our layover hotel, the Hilton on George St, but she was slated to perform at the hotel ballroom for three nights during our layover. Even though the shows had been sold-out well in advance Miss LaBelle told us, "Don't you worry children, Patti will take care of y'all" assuring us that we would all be front-row centre stage on the second night of our stay. Every member of our crew was elated, eagerly anticipating our good fortune in being able to enjoy a performance of the legendary Patti LaBelle in such a close-up and personal manner. Before dispersing to our separate rooms, we all chipped in to buy a huge floral bouquet as a token of our gratitude for the kindness and generosity bestowed upon us by this true super star.

I was deep in slumber trying to overcome the effects of crossing not only the international date-line but several time zones, when I was roused from my comatose state by the incessant ringing of the telephone. By now it was 1am and removing my ear-plugs but keeping on my eyeshades, I blindly fumbled for the receiver, almost overturning the lamp on the nightstand in the process, and groggily croaked, "Hello?" I had struggled to a semi-upright position in the bed when a deep, authoritative voice inquired, "Is this Mr Harris?" Not fully awake, I replied in the affirmative that, "Yes ... this is Mr Harris... What's up?" I wasn't fully paying attention, thinking to myself that this was a nuisance call and was about to hang-up the phone when I caught the phrase: "We would be honoured if you and a companion would join us for a complimentary dinner and show this evening." Upon hearing the words *complimentary* and *dinner* uttered in the same sentence, I sat up-right in bed and asked the person on the other end of the phone, "I'm sorry ...I didn't quite catch all of that.... Could you repeat that please?" The gist of the ensuing conversation was that I was indeed being invited, along with a guest, to a dinner and cabaret performance by David Campbell, an up and coming Australian performer, at 8 pm that evening.

Although I was not a local, I had a basic knowledge of who David Campbell was. The son of famous rock 'n' soul singer Jimmy Barnes, David was a rising star in his own right. A gifted vocalist and actor, he was forging a formidable reputation as a stellar cabaret crooner and I leapt at the opportunity to catch his act, although I was puzzled as to why I was being invited out for an evening's entertainment, as David Campbell's guest no less!

"Mr Harris. Will you be able to join us this evening?" the voice repeated. I hastily replied in the affirmative and hung up the phone.

By now wide awake I immediately called the room of Ann-Marie Berry, my dear friend, who as luck would have it, was flying with me on this trip. After groggily consenting to be my date for the evening, she agreed to meet me in the hotel lobby bar for pre-dinner cocktails at 7 pm. Just before 7pm, nattily decked out for an evening on the town, we strolled over to the concierge desk and stating the fact that I was Mr Harris, enquired if my name was indeed on the list of invited quests for David Campbell's show that evening. Having ascertained that this was in fact the case, Ann-Marie and I ducked into a taxi and headed off to the venue where David Campbell was performing.

Upon arriving at a luxurious wharf-side hotel, we immediately noticed that there was a considerable number of patrons lining up to enter the building. Stepping up to the front of the line and announcing, "I'm Mr Harris and I believe that I'm expected", we were ushered into the theatre and directed to a front-row table where the placard read reserved. After a light repast, the lights dimmed in the small, intimate room and David Campbell took to the stage. His performance was stunning! After a few introductory ballads he switched to his forte, Broadway show-tunes, which highlighted both his vocal range and his finely nuanced interpretations of classic tunes from a variety of Broadway shows.

Along with the rest of crowd Ann-Marie and I were mesmerized, joining in the thunderous applause after each song, however, we were thoroughly unprepared and pleasantly surprised when during the intermission between sets, David bounded over to our table, introduced himself and profusely thanked me for, "taking the time out of my busy schedule" to attend his show. I was utterly flabbergasted, thinking to myself, "Busy schedule, pouring coffee and tea?" and had opened my mouth about to say something to that effect when a sharp kick to my shins caused me to halt mid-sentence. Ann-Marie meanwhile demurely purred, "Oh, it was our pleasure", going on to state how much we had enjoyed his performance. When he left us to change for the second act, I still stammering and speechless, Ann-Marie turned to me and under her breath said, "He obviously has you confused with someone else.... but we've already drunk the man's champagne, eaten his food and got a command performance to boot....so just shut-up and enjoy the show!" The lights once again dimmed, the band struck-up and I nervously replied, "Yeah....but just who the hell does he think I am?"

The second half of the show was as thrilling and irrepressible as the first set and David closed out the evening with a touching, heart-felt rendition of *Mr Bojangles*, which brought the crowd to its feet. At the show's end, he once again came over to our table where both Ann-Marie and I expressed our appreciation for being invited, exclaiming what an incredibly talented performer he was. After autographing copies of his debut album *Yesterday is Now*, David once again thanked me for fitting him into my schedule, adding that he would be delighted if I could catch his debut in the US at the Rainbow Room in NYC that fall. Replying that I would be thrilled to do so, we parted company and Ann-Marie and I, still perplexed as to whom exactly I was being mistaken for, set off into the night.

The next morning, I was regaling the personnel at the front desk of the hotel with my unexpected windfall and adventures of the previous night when a well-dressed middle-aged African American gentleman cleared his throat from where he had been standing just behind me and intoned, "Aha. So you're the imposter!" Mortified, I slowly turned my head and was about to offer up some feeble response when he burst out laughing, "I'm kidding – really! I was just wondering who got to take in that show last night which I was too busy to attend in the first place. By the way I am Richard Harris from MCA Records and you are?" After introducing myself, "Tal Harris.....from United Airlines", he guffawed, adding, "Well that explains quite a bit Mr Harris." After I had described to him just how the mix-up had occurred, the other Mr Harris assured us that no harm had been done and we both enjoyed a lengthy laugh over what was clearly a case of mistaken identity.

That fall I managed to catch David Campbell's cabaret performance at the Rainbow Room in NY. While I wasn't able to obtain front-row seats (and didn't dare to go backstage), I was able to witness yet another star turn of the youngest person ever to headline that august venue - and to absolute rave reviews!

The next evening after David's performance in Sydney and as promised, our entire crew were guests of honour at Patti LaBelle's sold-out concert held in the Grand Ballroom of the Sydney Hilton. From the moment she stepped on stage Miss LaBelle was electrifying; strutting across the stage, belting out a repertoire of her many hit songs and ending the first half of her show with the iconic disco anthem *Lady Marmalade*, which had the entire audience on its feet, singing along and *boogying in the aisles*.

Before she left the stage to change costumes for her second act, she blew a kiss to our table acknowledging her, "lovely new friends, who took such good care of her and her entire entourage on her flight to Sydney!" Our table erupted in raucous cheers and shouts of, "We love you Patti!" as we joined the crowd in a standing ovation. By the finish of her concert, our hands were sore from wildly applauding, our throats raw from shouting our approval and we joined the whistling, wildly cheering crowd in bringing Miss LaBelle back for three prolonged encores. Patti finished the evening with an amazing rendition of, *You are My Friend* that once more brought the audience to its feet and she exited the stage to a full five-minute-long standing ovation.

That evening will long remain in my memory as one of the most sensational performances I have ever had the pleasure of attending and to this day I consider Patti LaBelle one of the most remarkably gifted artist to ever grace a stage or record a song.

There have been occasions when I've met someone whose face is so familiar to me that I've been certain I knew them, but couldn't for the life of me make the connection to just where or when.

About ten years ago I was returning to NYC after a two-week holiday in London where I had been catching up with old friends. I was lucky enough to have been assigned the last seat in the First Class cabin and had just finished stowing my carry-on luggage, when the gentleman seated next to me glanced up from the newspaper he had been perusing and politely nodded in my direction, allowing me a fleeting glimpse of a ruggedly handsome, weathered face that was vaguely familiar to me.

In the dim recesses of my memory I speculated that we obviously had crossed paths during the course of my flying career and, in fact, I was certain that we had worked a flight together in the not too distant past. Common sense should have intervened at this point and a lesson reverberated that was ingrained in my psyche by my 5th grade elementary teacher Mrs. Shipp, "Class, never ASSUME anything; it can only make an ASS of U and ME!"

Instead of heeding that advice from long ago and not wishing to be rude and stare while I wracked my brain attempting to place just where and when we had met, I thrust out my hand and decided to introduce myself, "Hello ... I'm pretty certain that we've worked together in the past. Aren't you based in New York? My name is Tal Harris!" With a quizzical expression on his face he hesitantly replied, "BASED? Yeah I LIVE in New York... I'm Al, AL PACINO!" The light bulb FINALLY came on in my head at the same instant I realized EXACTLY WHY the stranger's face was so familiar. Al Pacino was one of my favorite actors and for some ASININE reason I had equated that world-renown visage with that of a UAL CREW MEMBER!!!

Feeling like a complete idiot, I hastily withdrew my hand and in a small, slightly humiliated voice replied, "OHHH ...Oh YES... of COURSE! UMMM ...Pleased to meet you Mr Pacino!" Slinking down into my seat I spent the rest of the flight with my head buried in a book, praying to all the Gods that my faux-pas would not be increased by some random F/A coming up to me and asking, "Hey Tal...what trips are you FLYING this month?"

I was greeting passengers at the front entry door on a flight from MEL-LAX when I directed a long-haired, middle-aged man and his wife to their seats in the last row of the first class cabin. As he passed me I jokingly commented, "You know Sir... You could REALLY be a dead -ringer for Kris Kristofferson!" Smiling wanly, he gruffly replied: "Yeah I know, I get that reaction quite a lot!" The flight was completely full and as I was working business class with 40 demanding passengers, both the remark and the gentleman seated with his wife in 4C and H completely slipped my mind.

It wasn't until later in in the flight, when I ventured into First Class to offer sales from the duty-free cart, that I happened to glance at the seat chart posted on the galley wall. My eyes bugged out of my head when I noticed in bold italics the names; Mr and Mrs Kris Kristofferson! As I strolled to his seat with a sheepish grin plastered on my face I gathered he realized that I had discovered he was in the fact the real deal. He stretched out his hand and laughing said, "Hi... I'm Kris Kristofferson. This is my wife Lisa.... And YOU are?" Without missing a beat I replied, "Hello Mr. Kristofferson, my name is Tal and I've often been told that I remind people of the empty-headed scarecrow from the *Wizard of Oz*!"

We both enjoyed a chuckle at my expense and after that incident I made it a point to ALWAYS check the manifest before assuming anything at face value alone.

Probably the biggest gaffe that occurred in my flying career was thankfully not of my making. One of the most famous entertainers in Las Vegas, *Mr. Show Business* himself, Wayne Newton, was seated in seat 1K on the flight from LAX to LHR. Mr Newton was a thoroughly affable and extremely charming man, who kept quietly to himself, watching the occasional film and reading a novel to pass the time away. The seating on the 777 aircraft is such that seat 1K is directly adjacent to the galley in First Class, and although a curtain divides the main cabin from our work area, FA's have to maintain a modicum of quiet as every sound reverberates throughout the first couple of rows in the cabin and the slightest sound can be heard quite clearly.

I was working the aisle position and spent most of my time interacting with and serving the passengers seated in the First Class cabin. The junior girl who was working the galley position, was an exceptionally loud- voiced New Jersey native, with a brash clarion-like tone to her every utterance. Apparently, SHE was more focused on preparing the dishes for seats 1A, 2A etc and NOT looking at the names on the seating chart as she brusquely supplied me with each course to be delivered in the cabin. At one point after the dinner service was complete, Wayne Newton got up from his seat and proceeded to cross the aisle and past the galley on his way to the lavatory located on the left side of the plane. As fate would have it, just as he was rounding the corner to return to his seat my loud-mouthed co-worker barked out, "HEY...did you get a look at that guy with the jet-black hair??? He looks like a BAD WAYNE NEWTON IMPERSONATOR!" Mortified and certain that he had overheard her I loudly "SHUSSED" her, giving her a death-glare and making a ZIPPING motion across my lips at the same time! As soon as he was safely back in his seat I leaned in close to her ear and hissed in a stage whisper, "YOU IDIOT! That IS WAYNE NEWTON!" My tactless and outspoken galley girl gasped, "OH...SHIT!!!" and scampered back into the galley as fast as her stubby legs would allow!

The remainder of the trip passed with as little verbal contact as possible between the verbose *Miss Jersey* and myself and the service thankfully continued without further incident. Poetic justice was served however when we reached the gate and our passengers were deplaning. As I thanked Mr Newton for travelling with us and welcomed him to London, he turned to my flying partner, now standing next to me at the door, and smiling at her said, "You know...you REALLY should catch those Wayne Newton impersonators the next time you're in Las Vegas. I hear they're really TALENTED!" I fell out laughing as my loud-mouthed companion turned fifty shades of RED and fled into the bathroom!

CHAPTER 41
PRIVATE DANCER

I was thrilled beyond description to have met the incomparable Tina Turner on not one but two occasions. My first encounter with this living legend was in the spring of 1985 when she was headed down under to film George Miller's *MAD MAX: BEYOND THUNDERDOME*, the third instalment in the Mad Max film series. Miss Turner starred in the film along with MEL Gibson (reprising his role as Mad Max Rockatansky) playing Aunty Entity, the beautiful but ruthless ruler of the apocalyptic community called Bartertown.

As the chief purser on the crew, you're usually situated at the front door of the aircraft where the FC passengers board the airplane. The cabin was almost filled when I caught sight of a Red Carpet representative engaged in an animated conversation with a glamorously-dressed woman wearing a sexy black leather mini-dress, black bolero jacket, white silk blouse off-set with pearls and black over-sized sunglasses... all topped by a mass of tousled, blonde hair. When they drew nearer, my eyes widened in recognition of the immutable Tina Turner and my mouth widened in a huge, surprised smile. I had barely caught my breath and was still grinning like the village idiot when she clasped my outstretched hand with both of hers and purred in a raspy, sultry voice, "Good evening young man!" I stammered out, "Well...welcome aboard Miss Turner, may I show you to your seat?" She gave me a dazzling smile and linking her arm in mine, we proceeded to the front row of the plane and her seat 1A.

Every eye in FC was on the rock 'n' roll legend as she sauntered to her seat. I have to admit that I quite enjoyed being a momentary object of attention, if only by default, as the murmurs of, "IS THAT...? Oh my... she looks FABULOUS!" resounded throughout the cabin. Let me state for the record that her fabled legs were every bit as toned and terrific in 1985 as they are today, 30 years later!

Miss Turner was thoroughly charming, politely engaging her fellow passengers in First Class, who were as thrilled with her presence as I was. More importantly, her personality and lack of haughty arrogance, which is too common with many celebrities, was not only refreshing but made her physical beauty that more alluring.

At that point in her career, Tina Turner had been living in Switzerland for many years. When her young female assistant came up from business class to speak with her, I was impressed by her conversation in flawless, perfectly accented German. At the completion of our meal service, Miss Turner took the time to chat with the F/A's working that trip, and when the hubbub had subsided and we were alone, I found myself engaged in a conversation about her life and the journey she had undergone from her early days as Anna Mae Bullock from Nutbush, Tennessee, to the pinnacle of fame as Tina Turner.

Her life story was well known; her abusive marriage and early career with Ike Turner and her rise to fame as a solo artist. What I did not know was that the *queen" of rock 'n' roll* was a longtime Buddhist, having begun the practice during her turbulent marriage in the 1970s. Miss Turner explained to me that Soka Gakkai, the tradition to which she adheres, is a form of Nichiren Buddhism and that chanting (in Japanese) NAM-MYOHO-RENGE-KYO, roughly translated as The Mystic Law, gave her the peace of mind and the wisdom to deal with any situation and the ability to tap into her highest potential. She explained that by focusing on love and harmony, it allowed her to move forward in her life, channeling negativity into positive energy, not only for herself, but as a force of good for the world at large. Although I had been raised in the Catholic faith, I was never deeply religious, and I found myself more than a little intrigued by the powerful, peaceful tenets of her Buddhist practice.

In those days on the 747 aircraft, the crew rest area was in the rear of the aircraft in a compartment situated just underneath the plane's tail, which we entered via a staircase leading up to our bunk room. The sleeping berths were arranged like those on a train, two on each side, in a bunk bed fashion. As I laid my head down on the pillow in my upper berth bunk, I repeated the mantra NAM-MYOHO-RENGE-KYO... until I fell into a deep and peaceful slumber.

In the weeks following that particular flight, I found myself increasingly drawn to and captivated by this sect of Buddhism, reading everything I could regarding Buddhism, but particularly regarding the practice of Soka Gakkai, and soon found a group which practiced chanting near my home. After months of practicing the tenets espoused by Soka Gakkai and incorporating them into my life, I fully immersed myself in its philosophy and on October 15, 1985, became a Buddhist.

Four years later, I was lucky enough to once again have Tina Turner on a flight. This time she was travelling from LA to London to film an ad campaign for the opening season of the Australian Rugby League, which featured her mega-hit song *The Best*. She embraced me like an old friend and was utterly delighted when I told her that she had been the catalyst that had led me to seek fulfilment and tranquility in my life through the practice of chanting and Buddhism. At the conclusion of the flight, Miss Turner encouraged me to always follow the path of enlightenment that would inevitably allow me to realize my dreams.

It is not often that we encounter, let alone are so indelibly influenced by someone who is universally held is such high esteem. For all her kindness shown to me and especially for enabling me to embrace the positive energy of chanting NAM-MYOHO-RENGE-KYO, I will be forever grateful to this truly beautiful and thoroughly amazing woman.

CHAPTER 42

ZONA ROSA

As a group, the majority of F/As (myself included!) had undergone a radical change in the uninhibited, wild partying and drug use that had been tantamount to the makings of a good time while on a layover. This was due in part to maturity and outgrowing the need for recreational drugs, and quite a lot due to the introduction of random drug testing. Where we once might have spent 48 hours over-indulging in bowls of cocaine that cost a mere $20 in Caracas, Venezuela, we were now more prone to a stiff drink or two after a flight and eagerly looked forward to the restorative properties of a sound night's sleep.

Thus it was in the fall of 1994, that an older and definitely wiser version of me was working a flight to Mexico City from LA and had the Reggae group *BIG MOUNTAIN* on board. Their cover of Peter Frampton's hit song *Baby I love Your Way*, remade as a Reggae anthem, had climbed the charts, reaching the Bill Board Hot 100 at number 6. The lead singer Joaquín *'Quino'* McWhinney, bass guitarist Lynn Copeland and the rest of the band members, Tony Chin, Carlton *'Santa'* Davis, Michael Hyde, Billy *'Bones'* Skoll and James McWhinney commandeered the First Class cabin, in the process turning a routine flight into a full- blown party!

The group was on its way to perform a series of concerts and when we discovered we were all staying in the same hotel the entire cabin crew was invited to attend a concert as their guests of honour. Unfortunately, our 31-hour layover conflicted with the schedule of their first performance so we were invited to attend the sound-check and dress rehearsal instead.

The evening began at an up-scale restaurant located near the Paseo de La Reforma and fuelled by a fantastic meal and several pitchers of margaritas we decided to hit the bars and sample the nightlife of

Mexico City's notorious Zona Rosa. At some point in the drunken revelry that ensued, we found ourselves politely escorted out of a rather disreputable establishment for creating a scene when we danced on the tables while other, less inebriated patrons watched on in feigned disgust!

Several large bottles of tequila later, we finally stumbled into the complex where the recording studio was housed. I'm not certain just how they managed, but Big Mountain were consummate professionals, toasted or not, and they set about fine-tuning their instruments and after a nod from their sound engineer began to play. They were amazing even though it was now well into the wee hours of the morning and these guys performed as if four hours of hard core drinking and partying were an everyday occurrence.

At some point during the night, myself and three of my flying partners found ourselves with headphones on in the sound booth with the band, bellowing out the chorus:

"OHH Baby, I love your way... every day
Wanna tell you I love your way, every day
Wanna be with you night and day!"

I'm certain that the sound engineer more than earned his salary that raucous, rowdy night trying to compensate for the discordant brawling of my crew while supervising the recording of the band. We may be many things to many people, however professional singers (or singers AT ALL in my case) cannot be added to that august and ever-expanding list!

It was around 8am when we finally staggered out into a blinding sun and headed back to our hotel in order to catch a well needed nap before our return to LA late that same evening. We may have been red-eyed, bleary and a bit hung-over but as we hummed "OHHH BABY..." throughout the thankfully short flight home we all carried fond memories of a night none of us would soon forget.

The Crocodile Hunter – Aussie icon Steve Irwin

The William sisters on their way to Wimbledon

Andre 2000 of OUTKAST

Keith Urban – Country star

CHAPTER 43
STRANGERS IN A STRANGE LAND

A lot of the everyday occurrences or part of the daily news cycles we have become immune to in the United States can be quite alarming to tourists visiting our country from abroad. I was hosting my friend Paul Solomon from Melbourne for two weeks and set about treating him to an insider's view of the City of Angeles not usually experienced by tourist to our fair city.

Unfortunately for Paul, his holiday almost became a new wave Cinema Verite.

We had covered all the usual Hollywood and beach venues (Venice, Santa Monica and Malibu) and had spent a pleasant afternoon at my cousin Dan's Hollywood Hills home, which was located just below and adjacent to the famous Hollywood sign. We then decided to have dinner at a local eatery, Roscoe's House of Chicken and Waffles, a Southern California institution renowned for its *soul food*. Paul, who had become quite proficient and confident driving on the "wrong side" of the road, was navigating his way to the restaurant when he pulled alongside a late model black SUV, a Cadillac Escalade, at a red light traffic stop. We were in the midst of some mundane conversation when Paul suddenly halted whatever he had been saying and blurted out in alarm, "HOLY SHIT Look At the dude next to us!"

Being a native of LA and not wishing to draw attention to either of us, I casually glanced out the open passenger window and immediately noticed a metallic small calibre handgun blatantly placed on the seat next to the driver of the SUV, which had now drawn directly alongside of and parallel to our vehicle with its windows also open. Given the fact that the driver, a heavily tattooed Hispanic man in his late 20s, cigarette dangling from his mouth, wasn't paying attention to us, but was apparently up to no good, I whispered to Paul out of the side of my mouth, "Let's get the FUCK OUT of here!" Sure enough as soon as the light turned green and the Escalade took off, Paul deliberately lagged a few feet behind the vehicle and abruptly made a sharp right hand turn onto the next street. After sitting parked for a few minutes, allowing more than enough time to put some space between us and the shady character in the SUV, we set out once again for the restaurant. We arrived at Roscoe's only to discover the parking lot was filled to capacity so we parked in the next block and proceeded on foot. The fact that the parking lot was filled to capacity was nothing out of the ordinary as Roscoe's was extremely popular and was busy on a daily basis. The main dining room was obscured from our view by a panel at the receptionist's desk but we were soon ushered to a table for two in the middle of the restaurant.

There was, however, one major hiccup with our seating arrangement.

Apart from Paul's being the sole WHITE FACE in a packed venue of black and brown patrons, we apparently sat on the line of demarcation between two notorious and quite disgruntled rival GANGS: the Crypts and the Bloods. On either side of us sat burly, glaring, cantankerous thugs clad in either denim or leather, and each wearing a bandana declaring their gang affiliation - Red for the Bloods, Blue for the Crypts. In a move that would have made a magician proud, Paul alighted from our booth and smoothly back-pedalled to the relatively safe zone of the receptionist's desk, all the while announcing that we had changed our minds... and would be getting our meal... to GO!

The second our food was delivered, we both headed off at a brisk trot back down the block to our parked car. As we peeled away from the curb and were headed safely back to my house Paul turned to me and said, "Mate, I'm not sure what was about to go down in that place, but I'll be damned if I was going to be the feature story on the 10 o'clock NEWS!"

Apparently, life in the fast lane, or ending up in the line of fire was not high on his list of *Things to Do in LA!*

The next set of cultural misadventures occurred when another set of friends of mine from Melbourne, Justin and Paul Cougar, decided to make the de rigueur journey to the States and make their mark on California and LA in particular.

The Cougar brothers had determined that the only sensible mode of transportation while visiting LA was in a souped-up convertible and with this in mind rented a 2011 Mustang V6, which produced 305 hp and was capable of going from O to 60 in 5.1 seconds. I mention this only in passing, as to the best of my knowledge, neither brother had ever driven in the States and after passing up my offer to collect them at the airport in my Jeep Liberty (FAR too ordinary!) decided to imitate La Vida Loca and navigate the streets of LA on their own.

It was not without some trepidation on my part that I gave them directions to my house in the Mid-Wilshire district of LA (between Beverly Hills and West Hollywood) and wished them luck. My house was already prepared for their visit and knowing that it takes about half an hour to get from LAX to my front door, I began watering my front lawn while keeping an eye out for the white Mustang convertible they had described to me. I live in an extremely quiet residential neighbourhood with several middle schools and the children that populate them in the immediate vicinity. Thus it was with a mixture of anxiety, quickly followed by abject dry-mouthed FEAR, that I first heard, then spotted, a roaring mustang convertible; top down, music blaring, speeding towards and then THROUGH the intersection AND a stop sign of the street, where I now stood frozen on the spot, wildly gesticulating and screaming, "STOP..STOP" at the top of my lungs!

When the car had sped past me and Phil, the madman who at been at the wheel, realised he had over-shot his target, he screeched on the brakes and reversed at full speed back to where I stood THUNDER STRUCK! A scene followed in which I was hopping up and down like a mad hornet abusing them both with a profanity-laced litany on speed laws, highway safety and reckless driving in particular.

It was now mid-morning and fortunately all of my neighbours were either at work or at school. When the noise of the car had abated, my shouts of, "ARE...YOU...CRAZY!?" reverberated loudly throughout the block. After this tirade I finally relaxed, caught my breath and, after obtaining not only the keys to the mustang, but a solemn promise from them NOT to drive like maniacs, welcomed them into my home!

Later on in the day, when they had both proved themselves capable of driving like model citizens, we set out on a tour of Beverly Hills and Hollywood, while I sat in the back seat and gave directions...like a reversal of roles in the film *Driving Miss Daisy*.

Aussies, in general are an irreverent, boisterous species and when gathered in a group of two or more they create an instant carnival atmosphere, no matter the place or situation. Add alcohol to the mix and you have the recipe and excuse for outrageous behaviour.

The Cougar brothers were no exception to this rule of thumb...as I found out a few nights into their visit. To celebrate the official start of their holiday and to introduce them to authentic Mexican cuisine, I took them to El Coyote, my favorite eatery in all of LA. I have been dining there for years and as a consequence was known by the entire staff and was given VIP treatment whenever I stopped in. On the night of Justin's and Phil's inaugural visit El Coyote was filled to capacity, but we were ushered to a prominent booth in the centre of the main dining room. After receiving hugs and kisses from Maria, not only a dear friend but the best waitress in town, I ordered a round of double Cadillac margaritas, a tequila-based cocktail made with copious amounts of tequila, grand marnier and lime juice. Like everything Australians do, the boys knocked down the first round of drinks (which as I stated were DOUBLE the usual amount of alcohol) with gusto and ordered seconds. This was all before we had ordered anything to eat to curb the effects of a drink that could curl the toes of your average human being! By the time the second round of margaritas arrived the boys were feeling absolutely no pain. As their inhibitions lowered, the tone of their voices rose to full-throttle party mode, to the point where they could be heard quite clearly above the din of the surrounding patrons.

Just as Maria was about to place the large tray containing our meal she was precariously balancing down in front of us, Justin was concluding an anecdote regarding a recent encounter with a rudely unpleasant sales clerk. As he enthusiastically shouted, "....And you should have SEEN the look on that CUNT'S face when..." Maria almost toppled over with shock, her eyes as wide as saucers, and the over-laden tray gave a momentary wobble, while the entire room went suddenly as quiet as a morgue and every face in the immediate vicinity whipped around with an undisguised look of distaste glaring in our direction. I mumbled a quick apology to Maria, who glanced back over her shoulder, gave the *evil eye* to Justin as she beat a hasty retreat from our table. When the noise level once again rose and the last of our disapproving neighbors had returned their attention to their food, I hissed at Justin through clenched teeth, "DO...NOT ...EVER...USE that WORD in PUBLIC AGAIN!" I hastily explained that while the *C* word was casually bantered about in *OZ* ...it was ALWAYS frowned upon, in any circumstances (especially in mixed company), in the US!

After yet another round of drinks, which left each of us completely inebriated, all was forgiven and Maria's temporary displeasure was assuaged with an extremely generous tip, and we tumbled into a taxi making our merry way home.

On our return from the obligatory visit to Disneyland, while stuck in rush hour traffic, the boys spotted the Citadel Mall off the Santa Ana freeway. The fanciful 1700-ft-long facade resembles a set from D.W. Griffith's silent film spectacle *Intolerance*. The building itself is a replica of an Assyrian palace, replete with battlements and towering walls incised with giant Babylonian warriors and griffins - mythological creatures with the body of a lion and the head and wings of an eagle. The original edifice, which was built in 1929, housed the Samson Tire and Rubber Co and its design was a nod to the purported strength of the biblical character of Samson.

After a $50 million renovation, the building was re-invented as a 35-acre shopping mall. I had driven past this curious looking building many times and upon discovering that it was in fact a shopping emporium readily agreed to check it out.

The three of us set out the next morning to explore the Citadel and shop till we dropped. I knew that the mall was located between Downtown LA and Anaheim and figured that it should be fairly easy to locate. Unfortunately for us, in our haste to hit the road, we had all left our smartphones on the dining room table at home, and as a consequence, didn't have access to any form of directory or navigational assistance. In any event we figured that we would just drive southeast on the 5 Freeway until we spotted the unmistakable facade of the Assyrian palace.

The traffic flow on the Santa Ana Freeway is horrific at the best of times and on this day, we were barely crawling along at five miles per hour! By consensus we opted to get off the freeway and by keeping parallel with the highway we figured we would eventually reach our destination. This proved to be the biggest mistake of the day. Somehow we had taken an off-ramp that led us further east and away from any recognizable landmarks that would indicate just where in the hell we were headed. Instead we found ourselves deep in the WORST possible section of East LA; a neighborhood notorious not only for gang activity and violent crime in general, but known to harbor outright hostility towards trespassers.

In hind-sight, we must have looked like complete idiotic tourists; two white boys and a preppy-looking black man in a brand new Mustang convertible, trying our damnedest to look as inconspicuous as possible ...and get the hell out of Dodge! At one point we were hedged between two souped-up low-rider cars, one a bright purple 1978 Chevrolet Impala, the other a metallic green Buick Rivera, both filled with *tatted-up* locals, who obviously were wondering just what the fuck WE were up to! We sat quietly, desperately attempting to look as hard-core as we could muster, while the occupants of the cars operated their hydraulic lifts, causing the cars to lift and drop several feet which made the cars seem less like automobiles and more like predatory hunters on the prowl. It was with great relief we observed both cars peel away from the lights leaving us shaken...and scared shitless!

We spent the better part of an hour attempting to make our way back to the Santa Ana Freeway and after communicating using mangled Spanish and English, we FINALLY caught sight of the Babylonian palace again. Unfortunately for us, our *detour* had left us with very little time in which to shop, but by this point we were quite frankly relieved to have arrived in one piece, without suffering either grievous bodily harm or being robbed of all our earthly goods. After a cursory inspection of the mall, we decided to call it a day and without straying from the relative safety of the 5 Freeway we headed back home, crawling at a snail's pace the entire way without a peep of annoyance from any of us.

Justin seemed to have a knack for being overheard and misconstrued everywhere he went, and at one point he almost had his ass handed to him because of his use of an Aussie colloquialism.

To make up for our lost opportunity of retail therapy at the Citadel, we decided to stick closer to home and spend the day at the Grove, a trendy outdoor mall located in the Fairfax district of LA. There were major sales going on at the time, so every venue was filled to capacity with shoppers eager to snag a bargain. We were no exception, so that by the time we had reached the final stop on our expedition both Justin and I were weighed down with an accumulation of shopping bags of every dimension.

We were in a long line in *ZARA* waiting to pay for our goods, when Justin, speaking loudly so that he could communicate with me over the din of the crowd, mentioned that he needed to pick up a few *wife beaters*, an Aussie slang terminology for sleeveless tee-shirts or singlets. As I said, the place was thronged with people eager to pay for their purchases and get back outside into the balmy California evening. Unfortunately for Justin, an imposing 6-ft-tall black woman, already irritated by having to wait in a bustling, crowded queue, had over heard the word wife beater during our conversation and placing one hand on her hip angrily declared, "SAY WHAAAT...? WIFE BEATER..?! Why you lil' ...I WISH you'd try that SHIT with ME!" As she stood glaring down at Justin over her sunglasses I hastily moved in between Justin and his Amazonian would-be assailant and piped up, "NO! NO! NO! That's NOT what he meant..." and proceeded to try and explain that he was actually referring to an article of clothing. Like a beleaguered attorney trying to get his client off the hook, I finally succeeded in convincing the still scowling and sceptical woman that: A. Justin had no wife to "beat" in the first place; and B. Australians truly had a crazy way of labelling clothing.

With a drawn out, "Um-Hmm" the lady calmed down and both Justin and I breathed a sigh of relief. When we reached the safety of the sidewalk I informed Justin that in the future, I would act as his interpreter of Aussie to Yank speech and by-pass any unnecessary miscommunication and possible ass beatings!

CHAPTER 44
BAT SHIT CRAZY

The dastardly horrific attacks on 11 September 2001, changed the nature of air travel forever. In the aftermath of those acts of terrorism airports became more akin to maximum security facilities with armed guards, metal detectors, full body scans and checkpoints, turning a leisurely experience into one fraught with stress and overwrought nerves. Along with ramped-up security and aircraft that bear more resemblance to public transport buses than the spacious, comfortable cabins that were the norm in years past, people have completely lost the art of civility or tolerance with one another causing each flight to become a test of endurance.

After several decades of up-close and personal observation, it is my opinion that air travel today has led to a total loss of all rational thought processes. Perhaps it is an overabundance of negative stimuli with teeming masses constantly moving through luridly-lit air terminals, or being crammed ass-cheeks to jowls in an aluminium tube hurtling through space at 575 mph at 39,000 ft that is the correlation between the utter loss of common courtesy - or even common sense – experienced when dealing with fellow passengers in the confines of an aircraft cabin.

Passenger misconduct has become a daily occurrence and the nightly news has become filled with some of the more insalubrious actions of people, who seemingly check in their brains along with their luggage when they travel by air. While I have not personally encountered someone as out of control as the high ranking business executive who felt it was his prerogative to defecate on the serving cart in First Class on a UAL flight from South America to JFK, I have had more than my share of passengers who could rightfully be construed as certifiable nut-cases!

On a flight from LAX to SYD last summer, I was working the business class cabin with one of my favourite flying partners Dorie Cuttler, a witty, diminutive blonde purser, who does not suffer fools, or drunks for that matter, lightly. All was going smoothly until one of the F/As working the last section of the economy cabin dashed into the business class galley breathlessly demanding that, "Both of you, come quick!" Sensing some imminent disaster, we both took off at a brisk trot; Dorie down the right-hand aisle, I down the left. When we got to the aft galley, we were confronted with a screaming, red-faced Australian man in his mid-30s, his face contorted in an apoplectic rage. After Dorie had finally been able to calm him down and make sense of his ranting, we were able to discern that A, he was traveling with his wife and two small children (aged five and seven) and that B, the couple seated directly behind them in the middle seats were engaged in full-blown intercourse; the woman's legs and the heels of her feet knocking the back of his startled wife's head.

As soon as the words left his mouth both Dorie and I bolted out of the galley and down each side of the plane simultaneously arriving at row 37, when my eyes bulged out of my head upon catching sight of the hairy ass of a middle aged man furiously straddling a dishevelled glassy-eyed blonde in her early 20s. Her legs were spasmodically kicking the seat and indeed the head of the outraged Aussie's wife. Both of the culprits appeared not only thoroughly intoxicated or drugged but completely oblivious to the horrified onlookers on all sides of them.

Dorie might only be 5'2" tall but with the voice of a drill sergeant she bellowed out, "WHAT ...IN ...THE ...HELL?!" and, with a grip that would have done Arnold Schwarzenegger proud, grabbed the lothario by his belt, dislodging him from his barely coherent partner, while I assisted in dragging him to the aisle. Wrapping them both in blankets, we frog-marched them to the back of the plane where Dorie proceeded to not only interrogate the pair, who had never met before being randomly seated next to each other, but came down on them like the wrath of God!

The male culprit, his pants hastily drawn back up, drunkenly claimed that they were, "just making out" while the still dazed and bedraggled hussy claimed that she was "on medication" and "didn't remember a thing." Upon further questioning, it was revealed that the pair had been mixing alcoholic beverages with Ambien (a sleeping pill), a volatile combination in any situation, but which at 39,000 ft not only adversely affects your inhibitions but your judgment (and in this case morality) as well.

After profusely apologizing to the family who had been subjected to this pornographic display as well as to the passengers in the immediate vicinity of the amorous couple, we separated the two offenders informing them that they would be met by the Australian Federal Police upon landing. Sure enough, the moment the doors were opened, four burley Aussie cops, who all appeared to be former rugby players, hand-cuffed and dragged the now somewhat sober man unceremoniously down the aisle, while two female officers did the same to his now sobbing female companion.

The brazen couple were charged with "an act of lewd conduct and an act of public indecency", jailed and given a hefty fine, as well as being banned for future travel on UAL for life. While I've had passengers who became members of the *Mile High Club* in the past, those hormonally challenged individuals at least had the sense of mind to conduct their high-jinx in the confines of the lavatory (as unsavoury as that might be) and out of sight of their fellow travellers. Like the character of Nathaniel Hawthorne's novel *The Scarlet Letter*, I propose that all passengers who cross the line of acceptable behavior be forced to wear a flaming red letter "A" ... for "ASSHOLE"!

It is an unfortunate fact of life that most of the flying public has been immersed in a culture that fosters disrespect. As a product of a society that places more value on the individual, in particular getting your own way at all costs regardless of the consequences or the affect individual actions can have upon others, we've become tone deaf and callous to the needs of others. Our social network panders to the glorification of self to the exclusion of the group and as a result we now have plane-loads of self-centred, self-important cretins demanding that their every whim be catered to, no matter how ridiculous or outrageous the requests.

Since there hardly exists any respect or even courtesy for others, it is no wonder that F/As are confronted with passengers who have long ago forgotten that we are safety professionals first, and that the amenities, such as meals or drinks are primarily to provide a comfortable environment in which to reach your destination SAFELY. For some unknown reason, screaming and throwing temper tantrums more suited to nursery school than on airplanes, has sadly become the norm.

During the breakfast service on a SYD-LAX flight, a 60-something-year-old man started yelling obscenities at my flying partner Victoria Wolmort, because she had run out of cereal, his first choice of meal, and she had offered him an omelette instead. This nut-case was ranting ad-nauseum about, "How could this fucking airline operate without providing 100 per cent of its important passengers' needs" (meaning himself of course) and badgering Vicky. I was working the opposite aisle from this ass-hole and simply couldn't take another moment of his blustery bullshit. In my best imitation of James Earl Jones as Darth Vader I bellowed, "ENOUGH! Lower your voice ... HOW DARE YOU SPEAK TO HER LIKE THAT! If you've got a problem with catering write a letter to corporate headquarters... but do ...NOT ABUSE the F/A!"

You would have thought the voice of God had parted the heavens because the entire cabin went so silent that you could have heard a pin drop. The screaming idiot sank back down into his seat, his face flaming red and looking like the complete ass he so obviously was. His wife, thoroughly embarrassed by his behavior, whispered something in his ear and he meekly accepted the omelette that was now placed in front of him. The rest of the passengers in the cabin, who had been witness to both his outburst and my commanding response, gave me approving nods and returned to their breakfast as if nothing untoward had occurred.

Elderly white males are the worst offenders of bad behavior, in particular old white men returning from cruises. There is a saying among F/As that the only people who go on cruises are "the newly wed and the nearly dead!"

On a recent flight from SYD to LAX, I was confronted with a belligerent man in his 80s who apparently still thought he was on board the ocean liner (with a ratio of eight staff to one passenger) who brusquely shoved his steak precariously close to the edge of his tray, braying that this was the WORST meal he had ever SEEN in his entire life and demanding some REAL food in its place. Mind you, he hadn't even bothered to TASTE the proffered steak, the mere sight of it was enough to set him off to make a judgement regarding the taste. Without batting an eye and lowering my voice, I turned to his wife and in a calm, cool and collected manner said, "When your husband finishes his little tantrum, inform him that I understand the pasta is quite edible today!" ...and casually sauntered off down the aisle.

The "PRIZE" for histrionics however must assuredly go to a woman travelling with her seven-year-old son in the economy cabin on a flight from Shanghai to LA. I was sitting in the rear of the plane across from Peter Jackson, who was working the aft galley. As we had just begun the take-off roll down the runway, we were both securely strapped into our jump-seats. The plane had started to ascend and the wheels had yet to retract into the belly of the plane when a rabidly hysterical Chinese woman in her mid-30s began running towards Peter's jump-seat, screaming at the top of her lungs," MY BABY, MY BABY...! He need OJ...NOW!" At this point the aircraft was at a steep 45-degree angle due to the fact we were still rapidly climbing to our cruising altitude. Peter yelled over the engines roar, "Madam, it's NOT SAFE for you to be out of your seat!

Return to your seat and fasten your seat belt NOW!" The crazed woman continued towards Peter until she was directly in front of his face, all the while shrieking in a mixture of Chinese and mangled English, "MY BABY...YOU GIVE HIM OJ...NOW!" In tones that were reminiscent of a Chinese opera singer, her voice rose in a continually higher octave as she repeatedly screeched, "BABY...OJ ...NOW!" until she had worked herself into a histrionic full blown tantrum. Unfastening his seatbelt Peter stood up, towering over the shrieking mad-woman and pointing his arm in the direction of her seat, informed her in no uncertain terms that if she didn't comply and return to her seat immediately he would inform the captain, forcing us to return to Shanghai, off-loading both the crazed woman and her baby, as well as charging her with the bill for the fuel we had burned up due to her altercation.

While this drama unfolded, I had notified the purser via the inter phone to these events, who eventually joined Peter in escorting the now thoroughly over-wrought, wailing, hysterical hot-mess back to her seat, where her son looked on, completely non-pulsed by the drama his mama had caused.

The *one child* rule in China has created a culture in which that one child is raised and treated like an emperor or empress, and this crazed woman was no exception. It turned out that her seven-year-old baby's ears were blocked and instead of ringing her call-button to ask for assistance she had taken it upon herself to deal with the situation in a full blown panic. The son had made a miraculous recovery and was now nonchalantly staring out the window, while his overly emotional mama sat with great chest-heaving sobs in her seat.

As we began to return to our jumps seats I turned to Peter and in a voice loud enough to be overheard by everyone in the vicinity declared, "It appears that she has become UN-HINGED!" Assessing our now silent woman I smiled and addressing the passengers seated around her murmured, "Do let us know if she has another fit, won't you?" and we proceeded on with our duties.

While I'm on the subject of craziness, I'd be remiss if I failed to mention a few of the things that drive F/As absolutely bonkers! While we do realize that many passengers, especially our business class customers, do travel quite frequently, it absolutely irritates the hell out of us to be told, "I probably fly more than YOU!" (Trust me on this... you DON'T) and proceed to adopt a pompous attitude regarding our inflight duties. Most maddening are the loud, brash ass-holes who seem to be in a shouting match with their seatmates, loudly braying over the volume of the safety video or live demonstration. Believe me, it's far better to adopt an air of insouciance and keep your trap shut for three minutes than to annoy the crap out of someone who just may have to haul your arrogant ass out of the aircraft in an emergency situation.

It's always best to obtain the attention of crew members with a polite, "Oh Miss or Sir" rather than by grabbing an article of clothing, tugging on a serving garment, or even worse, patting or touching our rear ends as we pass by. Not only will this elicit a universally hostile response and a tart reprimand from the offended crew member, it virtually guarantees that your request will be delayed, if not outright denied.

Do not expect your F/A to stow a carry-on bag in which you have somehow managed to cram 100 kg of your worldly possessions in the over-head bin. A good rule of thumb in this regard is if you were able to drag it on board, you can summon the strength to dead lift your hefty suitcase into the overhead compartment on your own.

As difficult as this may be, try to figure out what your beverage of choice would be before your F/A reaches your seat. Every time I ask a passenger, "What would you like to drink?" and their response is, "What do you have?" I'm tempted to retort, "Oh, I don't know, about 120 people in back of you that already know what they're going to drink! …Now what do you want!"

Please manage to house train your under-age offspring before bringing them on a long-haul flight. Nothing is more aggravating to FAs than the constant pitter-patter of the little feet of squalling, squealing, snotty-nosed brats dashing down the aisles in between the serving carts as we attempt to do our job. While we can lay claim to being inflight barkeeps, food servers and occasionally bouncers, *Nanny Service* is never included in the price of your ticket.

Good hygiene goes a long, long way in creating a pleasant atmosphere and environment on an aircraft. A simple shower and deodorant can alleviate the horror of spending hours in a confined space sitting next to someone whose fetid breath, rancid body odour and foul-smelling feet render breathing impossible. I have lost count of the number of times I was forced to hold my breath like a competitive deep-sea diver in order to pass through the cabin!

Bringing your own supplies with you can also make your flight more endurable. In this age of bottom-line market shares and cutbacks in on board amenities, even pillows and blankets have become scarce. Baby food, diapers or nappies, eyeshades, earplugs and even toothbrushes have become things of the past in the main cabin. As I pleasantly informed a South African passenger who enquired if we had any "shampoo, toothbrush and deodorant on board", "Sir this is a 777.... I believe that what you're looking for is a 7-11!"

While noise-cancelling headphones are a boon to traveller's eager to block out the ambient drone and chatter on an aircraft, they are without doubt the bane of F/As everywhere. There is absolutely nothing so frustrating than standing face to face with a passenger who stares blankly at you when you're attempting to take either a drink or meal order. Here's a hot tip; if you happen to notice a F/A hovering over you and their attention is focused primarily on you at the same time their lips are moving, REMOVE your damn headphones if for no other reason than to find out what the hell they could possibly want.

Finally, try to exercise a modicum of patience when traveling on a commercial aircraft. If you can turn your head to the left and to the right of you and look in front and behind you and there are more than five people within your sight, this is a very clear indication that you are on a commercial aircraft and not your Gulf Stream G650 (the BEST private jet $65 million can buy). Adjust your attitude and sense of expectations accordingly and rest assured that your F/As will be with you just as soon as their duties permit.

CHAPTER 18
GROUND CONTROL TO MAJOR TOM

Crazed passenger anomalies are not limited to inflight incidents alone and I have had the dubious distinction of being eyewitness to more than a few of them. One of the more memorable moments occurred on a SYD to LAX trip, where Rita Helmsley, a former Pan Am stewardess who hailed from Finland, was the chief purser. I was working the business-class section on the upper deck of a 747 with one of my best friends George Rhinehart, a Chicagoan, who had one of the sharpest minds and quickest wits of anyone I have ever known.

The plane had just pulled away from the gate and the safety video was about to begin when the ALL-CALL chime sounded on the cabin inter phone. We both immediately stopped what we were doing and answered the phone, George in the galley located in the rear of the upper-deck, myself in the aisle. In heavily accented English Rita informed the crew that, "Ve vill be returning to the gate. Prepare for arrival. NOW!" After dis-arming our emergency exits (dis-engaging the door slides), I told George that I would go downstairs to the FC cabin where Rita was working to find out what the hell was going on.

I arrived on the scene just in time to witness two of *LA's finest men in blue* hand-cuff and escort an over-weight middle-aged man, his face contorted and flush with anger, screaming drunken obscenities at a completely calm, cool and collected Rita, as he was being dragged forcibly down the jet way away from the now open First Class doorway. When the din had subsided and a semblance of normalcy had returned, I approached Rita, who had stepped into the First Class galley to brush a strand of hair from her face and was composedly re-applying her lipstick, to inquire just what the cause of all the commotion was. Snapping her compact closed, she leaned in and intoned, "Dahlink that HORRID little man (who had been seated in front of her jump seat) wouldn't listen to me. When

I kept telling him that he must bring his seat upright and fasten his seat belt he kept yelling ...'FUCK YOU BITCH.... I DON'T HAVE TO LISTEN TO YOU!' When he continued cursing at me I called the captain and told him, 'Ve must return to the gate immediately'. When the nice policemen came and took him away I turned to him and said ... 'No I am NOT fucked, sir; YOU are fucked...YOU are being ARRESTED and going to JAIL!'"

George told me that he could clearly hear my uncontrolled outburst of laughter in the upper-deck galley as I literally bent double with laughter. The juxtaposition of our demure, refined purser putting down this over-bearing bully was priceless and an image that I will never forget!

When I bounded up the staircase to the upper deck, still chortling heartily, I saw George engaged in what can only be described as a lively discussion with an obtuse elderly man seated in the first row just behind the cockpit. By the time I appeared on the scene the man, frail and well into his 80s, was standing nose to nose with George, arms flailing like a windmill muttering, "Oh yeah?! You want a piece of this... hunh?! Come on ...BRING IT!" Apparently this ancient warrior, on his way to a cruise, had taken offence when George had asked him to return to HIS seat and buckle-up just moments after the debacle downstairs in First Class. George was doing his best to keep from laughing outright as he pointed out, "Listen buddy, we already have had ONE idiot arrested tonight ...You wanna JOIN him? Now SIT DOWN and fasten that seat belt... OR ELSE!" At that point the old man meekly complied, but sat bolt upright in his business class reclining seat, sulking like a three-year-old, neither eating nor drinking for the entire 14-hour trip to Australia.

When we got back to the galley and out of the passengers' view, George and I laughed until we had tears in our eyes, both surmising that all of the craziness on board that night had to be attributed to a brilliantly bright and bulbous full moon!

For the most part, the passengers who travel in business class are seasoned professionals, who operate by the karmic rule that dictates you interact with F/As with courtesy and respect (if not kindness!) resulting in a level of service that reflects their decorum. These types of passengers are a F/A's delight. They are either diligently working on a project or preparing a presentation and as a consequence eat, drink and maximize the amount of rest they can manage between meetings. On the opposite end of that spectrum are the overly demanding attention-seeking buffoons who, due to either an upgrade from mileage accrued or (very rarely) money spent on a full-fare ticket, assume that their newly acquired cachet entitles them to both use and abuse F/As they deem are on board to cater to their every (usually ridiculous) demands. We have an industry term for passengers who fall into this category; *Wanna be's* as in they REALLY want to be in First Class where they expect to be constantly pampered and fawned upon.

I was brought up to respect everyone equally, to treat a janitor with as much courtesy as I would a CEO, and I always welcome passengers as if they were guest in my home. There is however a limit to my tolerance for arrogant, obnoxious assholes determined to try my patience.

I was working the aisle of the upper deck business cabin on a 747 flight from LAX to SYD when I noticed a man in his early 40s struggling with several large pieces of carry-on luggage attempting to bring what appeared to be all of his worldly goods up the staircase. Even though I could tell at a glance he had exceeded the acceptable amount of carry-on luggage allowed, I bounded down the stairs saying, "Hello sir, let me give you a hand with that", at which point, without uttering a gracious "Thank You", he proceeded to un-load all but a small brief case into my arms. Knowing that I was going to be stuck with this charming character for the next 14 hours or so I figured that I'd start off on friendly footing and grunting with the effort, lugged his over-weight bags up the staircase, depositing them in the closet located at the top of the stairs. He lumbered past me and waddled his way to his aft-facing seat in the middle of the cabin. I had just finished stowing his suitcases when I looked up to see him stomping back down the aisle towards me with a look of disgust on his face. "This won't do at all!" he snorted.

"I beg your pardon sir...what are you referring to?"

"My seat is facing the REAR of the plane and I get NAUSEOUS flying sitting backwards!" I should point out that our business class cabin was outfitted with 20 rows of alternating forward or aft facing seats. Thinking to myself that even though every seat was comfortable perhaps this idiot truly suffered from motion sickness, I replied, "Sir, since we are completely full let me check with the gate agent, perhaps I can find you a forward facing seat in our downstairs business cabin." With a pompous nod of his fat, sweaty head, he indicated that I should do so and I set off to rectify the situation. A few moments later, I informed him that there was indeed a forward facing seat downstairs and that he was welcome to change seats. He shoved past me heading for the stairs and after taking a few steps turned to me and said, "Would you mind carrying my luggage down, I have a bad back" and without waiting for a reply, he stomped down the steps.

Flabbergasted, I glanced over at Derek Bainbridge my flying partner who was working the galley position and who like myself was African American and said, "What the HELL?! Does this ASSHOLE think he's on a friggin' PLANTATION?!" Derek, falling against the wall in laughter said, "Go on now.... lift that barge, tote that bale!" Defusing my mounting frustration with laughter, I decided that, "Screw it, we're better off to be rid of this bastard for the duration of the flight!" I shouldered his bags and began to drag his luggage, none to gently, banging and scrapping against the railway, downstairs to his new seat.

Derek and I had just finished serving pre-departure drinks and were tidying the cabin in preparation for the door closure, when the arrogant, rude prick we thought we had seen the last of, popped his head over the railway and barked, "I don't like that seat, it's too noisy and crowded down there ... I want my original seat back!" Evidently he had undergone a miraculous recovery from his previous condition, but I had experienced quite enough of his imperious attitude and was bound and determined to call him out on his bullshit and put an end to his obnoxious behaviour.

Walking to where he was standing on the stairway two steps below me I said, "Sir, may I see your ticket?" Clasping his ticket and pulling out my glasses from my jacket pocket with a theatrical flourish, I slid them down the bridge of my nose with my middle finger and after examining the document loudly explained, "AH.... I see the problem! Just here ... in the fine print. It clearly states, 'Lincoln FREED the SLAVES!'" The entire cabin erupted in raucous laughter as the man furiously snatched his ticket from my hands and crimson faced with humiliation stormed back down the stairs to his noisy, forward facing seat.

Later on in the flight as we were completing the dessert cart and were offering coffee or tea, Derek, who had just re-filled my silver serving pots, turned to me and said, "By the way...my sister got on ancestory.com and amazingly enough, found out the tribe in Africa our forebears came from." I replied: "Really? That's incredible!" Just as I was pouring a cup of tea and was passing it to the man on the aisle seat, he retorted, "Yeah man... It's the Motesuh tribe." Quizzically I looked up just as he replied, "That would be ... MO TEA SUH?!" I almost dropped the cup from my hand, spilling tea over the cart (but fortunately not over the passenger) as everyone within hearing distance fell about with laughter.

Not every episode of inflight craziness was the result of passenger misbehavior. This particular episode occurred on a 747 flight from LAX to SYD on the 10th anniversary of the downing of the World Trade Center on September 11, 2001. We were honored and privileged to count amongst our passengers a battalion of fire fighters who were the first responders to that horrific attack. When it was time for my rest break, I happened to be the last F/A to go upstairs to our rest area or bunk room as we called it. When I entered the darkened area, my first thought was that a light-bulb had malfunctioned as there appeared be a slight, grey haze in the small, confined space. However, by the time I bent down to enter the bottom, right-side bunk, I realized with a rapidly building sense of alarm that the haze in the air was actually a fine mist of SMOKE!

Any fire on an aircraft is cause for alarm and sensing that the source of the smoke must be emanating from someplace in the bunk room, I immediately roused the sleeping crew members by shaking them awake saying, "Get up, ...leave NOW!" as calmly as possible without letting the mounting fear I instinctively felt manifest that fact in my voice.

As luck would have it, one of the firefighters, a chief in fact, was standing near the door of the staircase when the now fully awake F/As bolted out. I instructed one of the crew to call the cockpit to advise them of the situation while I briefly and succinctly as possible explained what was happening to the fireman, who joined me in bounding back upstairs to ascertain if a fire emergency did in fact exist. Armed with a halon fire extinguisher, within seconds he confirmed that an electrical problem was the source of the haze in the air. By this time, a F/A arrived on the scene with a crash-axe to assist us in reaching the source of the fire, while another F/A stayed in communication with the cockpit via the inter-phone. When the fireman pulled back the curtain of the bottom bunk nearest the electrical panel to pry it open with the crash-axe, we both discovered our purser Elizabeth Patterson, clothed only in a Victoria Secret bra and thong, still sound asleep, on her stomach with her butt raised slightly in the air! Liz, I should add, was not only a yoga instructor and martial artist, but had an absolutely amazingly toned body. With a vigorous shake to her shoulder the firefighter shouted, "Hey ....you ...BOOTYLICIOUS, WAKE UP!' Liz's eyes flew open, and startled awake and no doubt in some shock to find a good-looking, well-built stranger hovering over her, she grabbed a blanket, squeezed out, "OHHHHH!!!" and fled down the stairs.

In short order, the fire professional had taken charge of the situation, danger was averted and a relative sense of calm returned to the crew. We were fortunate that this incident had occurred when the majority of the passengers were asleep and a situation that could have possibly gotten out of hand was averted. By now the entire crew was aware of our *sleeping beauty's* encounter with the handsome fireman and of the charming sobriquet he bestowed upon her. From that day on Elizabeth will forever be associated with the nick-name that best describes her; "BOOTYLICIOUS!"

Relieving stress with some close colleagues in a Tokyo noodle bar

After years of dealing with the public, you tend to develop a thick hide and a certain level of tolerance for moronic, rude behaviour from drunken passengers. Most people who tend to over-indulge in alcohol inflight are over compensating for a fear of flying or in hopes of falling asleep. Unfortunately, what is not common knowledge is that consuming one alcoholic beverage at 39,000 ft is the equivalent of three drinks on the ground. That being said, there is no excuse for overbearing, imperious treatment of F/As, ever!

On an LAX to JFK premium service early morning flight, an actor who had a prominent role in a cable television series was seated in the last row of First Class. A short, middle-aged man, sporting dark sunglasses with hair plugs attempting to cover a rapidly-balding pate, he was consuming Bloody Marys at a break-neck pace. The ground agent had informed me that he had been heavily drinking in the Red Carpet club prior to boarding, but had seemed to be "in control of his faculties and would most likely soon fall asleep... or pass out". With this information in mind I had been watering down his cocktails, merely floating a tiny portion of vodka on top of the Bloody Mary mix.

Every time I would pass by his seat, however, he would snap his fingers and without a word of, "if you please" or "thanks" to me, wave his empty glass in the air slurring:, "Another round!" His obnoxious behavior was annoying everyone in the First Class cabin and by the third time he barked out, "Another round!" I decided I'd had more than enough of his puerile attitude. Standing over him I said, "First of all, WHAT'S with the finger snapping?! Have you LOST your DOG??" In an alcohol-induced fog he replied, "HUH?...What???" Bending over and leaning in close enough to smell his putrid vodka-infused breath, I said, "Could you please remove your glasses... I'd like to see your face when I speak to you." He made a drunken attempt to comply, sliding his glasses halfway down the bridge of his nose. When I could see his blood-shot, dilated eyes I said, "What's up with the attitude? You're a TV actor NOT a POTENTATE! I've met TRUCK DRIVERS with better manners than you! CHILL OUT and give it a REST!" I received a thumbs up gesture and nods of approval from the passengers seated around him as I turned to walk away.

Within moments of our exchange the over-paid, over-indulged prick fell into a drunken slumber, loudly snoring for the duration of the flight.
When we landed in New York, I made a report to the ground staff regarding his behavior to prevent him from engaging in this appalling manner on future flights on UAL. Our drunken celebrity neither recalled nor acknowledged his loutish behavior as he stumbled off the plane and down the jet way and thankfully out of sight.

Our ground agents have the most difficult job in the airline industry. While F/As only have to put up with passenger misconduct for a finite period of time, unfortunately ticket and gate agent's face angry, frustrated and overly aggressive people on a daylong basis.

My dear friend Doris Knox, a ground agent at Sydney's Kingsford Smith international airport, regales me with tales of her misadventures at the check-in counter or the jet way, whenever we catch-up. My favorite anecdote of hers involves a woman who for some unknown reason was dressed in a nun's habit and had to be physically removed from an aircraft for noncompliance with the F/A's repeated requests to cease verbally abusing the inflight crew. She created quite a spectacle as she was dragged kicking and screaming obscenities, no lady, let alone a member of a religious order, would dare to utter.

Another was of the elderly Turkish gentleman, who, when asked if he had any over-sized bags to check, gave her a beaming smile revealing his two remaining canine teeth, framed by a bristling beard containing remnants of his last meal, and kept nodding and pointing to his uncomprehending, placid-faced wife!

I was witness to one of the most outrageous acts of passenger lunacy this past November when I was travelling from LAX to ORD (Chicago's O'Hare International Airport) on my way back home to Wisconsin for the Thanksgiving holiday. The week before Thanksgiving, always celebrated the fourth Thursday in November in the US, is usually the busiest period of air travel throughout the calendar year and this past season was no exception. Invariably the airports are overcrowded, overheated and the flights are oversold; the traveling public already in a rush to get to their holiday destinations are almost always in a foul and un-cooperative mood.

My flight to ORD was un-surprisingly overbooked, so I was grateful to take advantage of utilizing a jump seat, those uncomfortable flip-down seats FAs occupy for take-off and landing, usually the only time you will find us seated during a flight. I always compare sitting on a jump seat for any length of time to sitting on a rigid wooden church bench; bolt upright throughout a particularly long and tedious sermon. Given the fact that this is after all a free ride, however, you grin and bear it!

As a jump-seater, I was boarding the flight with the working crew when I overheard a heated, extremely contentious exchange between a scraggly blonde girl in her early 20s and the female gate agent in charge of boarding the aircraft. The agent was attempting to explain to the fractious girl that since this 737 was a smaller aircraft with limited storage space available for the completely-full flight, she would have to check her over stuffed roller-board suitcase to her final destination. With her voice rising in an increasingly acrimonious tone, the girl insisted that her bag travel with her, adamantly refusing either to listen or adhere to the agent's calm and completely reasonable request.

By now in hysterics, the unruly girl had attracted the attention of everyone in the immediate boarding area, and several passengers attempted to calm her down. Without batting an eyelid the crazed girl suddenly drew back her hand, balling it into a fist, and struck the agent who had been calmly speaking to her, with as much force as she could muster, in the throat. Everyone gasped in shock, but before the agent who was now clutching her throat in pain or her assailant could retreat, two airport policemen materialized as if out of thin air, wrestling the now startled girl to the ground.

In the mayhem that ensued, the stunned agent fell heavily against the podium she had been standing in front of before being assaulted, while her belligerent saboteur scuffled with the police officers who handcuffed her as she thrashed on the floor, loudly yelling obscenities at everyone within her sight. After the injured ground agent was attended to and the bedraggled, morose girl was led loudly sobbing away in hand-cuffs, a sense of stunned disbelief hung over everyone in the boarding area, the air buzzing with conjecture of what had just occurred. Five long minutes passed during which time a modicum of normalcy returned and the boarding process recommenced, this time with two agents handling the job of their injured colleague, backed up by the presence of a stern-faced airport police officer.

Not surprisingly, every passenger who boarded that flight to ORD readily offered to check their carry-on luggage without as much as a whimper of protest. During the four-hour trip to ORD I offered to speculate, along with the crew as well as most of the passengers, just what warped thought process would lead anyone to strike a person over something as trivial as checking an oversize bag, the consequence being not only a missed flight but a holiday most likely spent incarcerated in jail!

Not every instance of inflight mayhem is caused by humans, but sometimes rather by their four-legged companions. When I first started flying it wasn't unusual to have a service animal, usually a golden retriever or a German shepherd -accompanying a blind or disabled passenger on board the aircraft. With the advent of stress-related disorders or the slightest excuse for an idiosyncratic condition, comfort animals now share the cabin with the general public.

My personal opinion is that these often times hulking beasts masquerading as comfort animals are being transported in the main cabin because their owners cannot bear to relegate them to the cargo compartment and out of their sight for the duration of the flight. As an animal lover and the owner of a spoiled-rotten pooch myself, I can empathize with this sentiment, however the definition of comfort animal has burgeoned to ridiculous lengths. Sydney, my short, squat, 50 lb Staffordshire bull terrier, is positively minuscule in comparison to the hulking beasts I've encountered lately, all sporting a yellow or orange comfort animal vest.

Our inflight manual states that an animal as large as a Shetland pony may occupy the passenger cabin as long as they have been certified as being essential for the *well-being* of the passenger who accompanies it. While I have yet to encounter a pony, my eyes bugged out of my head when a nerdy looking man in his mid-30s boarded a trans-continental flight led by a shaggy-haired beast of burden, which upon closer inspection turned out to be a full grown Irish wolf hound. My consternation must have been obvious from the "W...T...F?" look on my face as the plaid-shirted, Birkenstock-wearing passenger pointed to his hound's orange vest muttering, "I suffer from shaking fits brought on by anxiety!" When I could close my mouth I mumbled, "Unhuh...OKAYYYY", all the while speculating just WHO would have to clean up the animal's horse-sized turds should nature run its course during the five-hour flight!

Apparently, it's not the size of the dog or the viciousness of their bite that poses the real threat to F/As.

On a flight from JFK to LAX recently, an elderly woman seated in the bulkhead dividing First Class from the main cabin, had to be physically removed from the plane because of her snarling and snapping Chihuahua. The dog, which clearly inherited its temperament from its vile, vulgar owner, was supposed to be sequestered in a pet-carrier at her feet. When the woman refused to kennel the seemingly rabid creature, a scuffle ensued involving FAs wary of having their digits severed by the snappy jaws of the little demon, and its overweight, heavily made-up owner, who screamed, "DON'T TOUCH MY DOG YOU BITCH" at the top of her lungs. Fortunately for the crew and the peace and tranquillity of the rest of the passengers, two of *New York City's finest* managed to corral the loudly yapping beast and handcuffed the profanity spewing crazed woman, dragging her un-ceremonially off the plane, presumably to a well-deserved jail cell!

As dramatic as that incident was, absolutely NOTHING can compare to what has to be the most outrageous case of comfort animal misconduct I have ever heard.

One of UAL's funniest, most beloved pursers, Kevin Centilla, left me in stitches when he stormed off a plane that had just landed from Newark, red-faced and still fuming with anger. When Kevin had calmed down enough to articulate the cause of his implosion everyone within hearing distance literally collapsed on the ground with laughter. In his thick Boston accent Kevin, who was well over six-ft-tall and built like an ox, bellowed, "Honest Ta GAWD... it was a FUCKIN' NIGHTMARE!"

The gist of the tale was that a woman seated in the business/first class cabin of the 757 was travelling with her service animal, a Capuchin monkey, which she had secured with a bejewelled collar and leash. Unfortunately the woman fell into a comatose-like slumber shortly after take-off loosening her grip on the leash. Kevin explained that every time he passed the monkey, "Its beady little eyes followed my every move... as if it were stalking me! When the plane began to descend the little fucker SCREECHED waking up not only its owner but the entire cabin as well. Startled, the old biddy let go of the leash and the goddamned monkey started hopping from headrest to headrest throughout the cabin. Now EVERYBODY'S awake and screaming, the monkey is barring its teeth and shrieking and I'm trying to corral the little fuck without gettin' BIT!"

Finally with the help of a resourceful man seated across from the flustered woman and her escaped ward, he was able to use a trench coat to scoop up and capture the creature. Somehow they managed to coax the monkey back into its carry-on kennel and into the custody of its now hysterical owner. Red faced and breathing heavily, Kevin and his crew succeeded in securing the cabin for landing, with Kevin all the while glaring with undiluted disgust at the caged and still shrieking monkey.

By the time Kevin had finished relating his mis-adventure to a crowd, which had hung on his every word, we all fell about like blithering idiots, tears running down our faces as we literally laughed our asses off!

CHAPTER 46
HOLDING PATTERN

Like anyone who has enjoyed a lengthy career at some point, you begin to focus on creating the next chapter in your life. In the airline industry, *seniority* is the determining factor not only in the quality of the trips you hold on a regular basis, but also dictates just when you can retire with enough guaranteed income to support you in your dotage.

Even though I have been flying for several decades now, I am competing for trips with F/As who have been treading the aisles for 50+ years with absolutely no intention of *hanging up their wings* anytime soon!

This situation was further exasperated by the bankruptcy filing of UAL on 9 Dec 2002. Consequently, our financial security was fatally jeopardized by the removal of our pension plan on 10 May 2005. The majority of our F/As, myself included, might have opted for retirement long before now, but the necessity of padding our 401K plans (a personal savings program) in order to enjoy a better quality of life in the future dictates working well into our *golden years*. While it's imperative that maturity and experience matter a great deal in this industry, the flip-side to this argument is knowing just when to make a graceful exit from the party.

The spectre of jet-heimers hangs over all of us and while I'm guilty of suffering bouts of *C.R.S* (can't remember shit), there are a few prime examples of F/As who have definitely lost the plot altogether!

Rose Patterson, a senior SFO F/A who had been flying for 70 years, commuted to San Francisco from her home in Seattle. On one occasion she arrived in SFO on the afternoon of her check-in for an international flight later that same evening. Unfortunately, the poor dear walked into the base domicile, checked her mailbox, turned around and got right back on the next flight to Seattle! When the crew desk rang her later that evening to ask her why she was late for work she replied, "But I already FLEW that trip!" I'm guessing that jet lag had finally caught up with her and in her addled state she assumed that was indeed the case.

On a LAX to SYD flight another *senior mama*, Suzanne Collins, left the bunk room at the conclusion of her rest break dazed and confused and walked the entire length of the 747 back into the business class galley. This in itself was not the issue; every F/A is slightly out of sorts when we first wake up. Unfortunately, Suzanne had forgotten to put on her uniform skirt and clad only in her blouse and cotton granny panties, had made her way through a darkened cabin filled with (fortunately) sleeping passengers! Taken aback by her appearance I asked, "UMMMM.... did you FORGET anything?" Thoroughly befuddled she nevertheless realized her garment was missing, but before she could turn around to retrieve her skirt I hastily offered to dash back to the bunkroom and spare her the indignity of a trip back down the aisle. In both of these instances the ladies involved were politely persuaded that it just "might be a good time to turn in their galley smocks and call it a day".

At this point in time, I am still enthusiastic about my job and look forward to each and every flight as the beginning of a new and potentially exciting adventure. I may not *party like a rock star* anymore and the *pills* I pop now are to alleviate aches and pains, but I still look forward to discovering new horizons.

If I get to the point where I can no longer recall if I have actually worked a trip or not, or report for duty not fully clothed, I like to think I would be cognizant enough to realize it would be in my best interest to keep my ancient ass on the ground!

When I contemplate what my life would have been like had I heeded the call of academia and ended up practicing Law, I'm fairly certain that I would have been successful in that field, but then I recall all of the events of my career inflight and I know without a shadow of a doubt that I would not have traded those phenomenal experiences for any other job on the planet.

I have travelled the world extensively, something that most people only dream of doing and in the process, encountered some of the most fascinating, incredible people in every profession possible.

I have been lucky enough to have been an eye-witness to some of the most momentous occurrences in the last four decades, all while working with the most amazingly gifted group of people I will ever encounter; and I have learned to truly appreciate the diversity of different cultures throughout the world, enriching my knowledge of the human condition in the process.

My life has been enriched by experiences no university or staid office job could ever have offered. That might sound a bit lofty, but how many lawyers can lay claim to that?

Made in United States
Orlando, FL
17 May 2022

17976909R00120